Under the Shadow II
The Full Story

THE STORY BEHIND THE STORY OF THE
12-YEAR PRISON SENTENCE
THAT DRASTICALLY TRANSFORMED
A LIFE

Anthony E Walton

Blessing

6/16/15

Under the Shadow II
The Full Story

Anthony E Walton

ISBN 0692256717
ISBN 13: 978-0-692-25671-8
Library of Congress Control Number: 2014912812
Mountain Top Publishing LLC, Paducah KY.

Produced by MOUNTAINTOP PUBLISHING, LLC
P.O. Box 7287 Paducah, KY. 42002-7287
mountaintoppublish@bellsouth.net

ACKNOWLEDGEMENT

Without a testimony the mercy of God would not be known to a dying world. I thank God for having a testimony and for His Mercy and Grace that inspired me to tell my story.

I thank God for my wife, Deborah, who went through many difficulties but remained with me from the beginning and has always been my greatest supporter and encourager.

Thank God for Bishop William Johnson for the prison visits and for baptizing me in Jesus' Name.

Very special thanks to Bishop Sherman Merritt for befriending me after prison, and have remained a supporter and friend.

Thanks to T5 Photography owner Titio Pratt, and Artistic Consultant Kim Hixon for the Book Cover design and to Marissa Majors for her editing advice.

Thanks to all my family and friends for all the encouragement and affirmation to write and publish this testimony.

TABLE OF CONTENTS

FOREWORD

Since my release from prison in May 1987, God has allowed me to inspire, encourage and give hope to many inmates and their families.

I've been privileged to give my testimony on the 700 Club, in jails, prisons, Churches and newspaper articles on numerous occasions.

God gave me the vision for The L.I.F.E. (Love Is For Everyone) Community Inc. a nonprofit organization of ministries catering to the needs of the community.

He has allowed me to produce a television program called "Life After Lockup," where I interview former inmates on their progression after incarceration.

The circumstances of the hardship I encountered, that helped to make me, were somewhat unique.

The Supernatural intervention of God throughout my incarceration was overwhelming.

I pray that in writing this book, the readers will also believe as I do. Regardless of the circumstances or conditions, if you turn your heart toward God, you too can be kept "Under The Shadow" of the Almighty.

Chapter 1

IN THE BEGINNING

THE EARLY YEARS

I was born on July 4 1957 in Kent County, Grand Rapids, Michigan at St Mary's Hospital at 3:15am. My mom and dad were separated at the time, so instead of giving me my dad's name, she named me after an actor from a movie she was watching at the time. I don't know where she got my middle name.

Evidently she and my dad got back together soon after, because my brother was born a week before my first birthday. He was the junior.

I was like the runt; I was pretty sickly and grew slowly. My brother was always bigger and could outdo me in almost everything. It really thrilled him to catch up with me every year in age, and I couldn't wait to get older every year just to keep him from passing me. They dressed us like twins and everyone thought we were.

I really don't remember a lot of my early childhood, just bits and pieces. I remember standing on a porch seeing my dad driving a green tractor in some very tall grass smoking a cigarette. I told this to my dad one day, and he said I must have been about two, because he remembered the green tractor and when he quit smoking.

I remember being in thick mud, on a very rainy night, walking to a red house and everybody left me. I got stuck in the mud and was crying, and my uncle Sam came and carried me to the house.

I don't remember a lot of laughter, but I do remember a lot of crying. Don't remember why, but I do remember crying a lot.

I remember chickens,.....EVERYWHERE!!

BEMIS, TENNESSEE

We moved to Bemis from Medon when I was about 5 or 6 years old because I started first grade from there. 18 Hunt Street was the address; I remember it was a duplex type house at first, and when the other family moved out, dad cut a doorway to connect the two sides.

I went to Rosenwald Elementary School in the first grade, and was terrified the first day that I was going to get left there. I saw a bus pull up through the window. I grabbed my lunch box, and ran out of the classroom in a panic before I was stopped by some of the older kids laughing all over themselves who let me know that it was the bus to take them to the high school.

I remember that I had some kind of groin issue. I had to wear some type of device, so I could not play during recess and had to stay close to the teacher when we were outside.

I really believe that the condition during my first grade year caused me not to develop proper leg strength when I should have been running and playing, but maybe not.

After the first grade, I guess I got better because I didn't have to wear that device anymore, however, the second, third and fourth grades were more of a nightmare than not being able to run and play. It was an all-white school down the street and around the corner from us that dad made us start going to.

My older sister, my brother and I and maybe two other Black kids were the only Blacks that went there. It was horrible! I think my brother and sister fought every day. I just cried, cried all the time.

J. B. Young was the name of the school, and because it was in walking distance, that's what we did. Most of the times the white people would sick their dogs on us so we had to run home, and guess who was always last? Fortunately we never got bit or caught.

I never understood why dad sent us there unless he thought we would learn racism head on. I couldn't figure it out at the time.

Dad had a temper. I was so afraid of him that I stuttered very badly. He would ask me a question and as I tried to answer, I would get hit or get a whipping for being stubborn or sassy.

That made me even much more afraid. I guess that aided me in accepting being bullied in school, because it was as if that was just how it was supposed to be for me.

Childhood was like a trap to me. Seemingly unable to escape, Dad and mom fought a lot, or dad fought mom a lot. Either way I was fearful that he was going to kill her or hurt her badly.

Dad worked rather hard, and we always had food, shelter and clothes, but he was very strict. Whippings were hard and fierce. Beatings and abuse is what they would be called today.

They always left marks and he would rub alcohol on the wounds sometimes when they bled. Sometimes we would be stripped up like little slaves after a beating.

We were not bad kids, just kids. There were six of us and we would always try to be extra careful when dad was around, but he seemed to always find some reason to get us.

I stuttered so badly I wouldn't talk much, especially when dad was around. Sometimes I could talk good and other times I couldn't get a word out at all.

THE NIGHT THAT CHANGED EVERYTHING

Although dad seemed mad all the time, he was very protective of us, maybe because we were so small.

One cold night, I was about 10 years old; we were playing tag outside with the kids from across the street. They were a little bigger than us but we always played together and no one ever got hurt, until that night.

Someone tagged me a little too hard and the back of my head hit a corner of one of the porch planks and I almost passed out. My head hurt something awful and I just sat down on the porch until they finished playing and we went in the house.

It felt like something was running down my face, so I asked my sister if she saw anything on my face. By that time, dad came out of one of the rooms and yelled "what happened?!" It scared me to death! I turned toward him, everything started spinning. He grabbed my coat and blood was all in my hood and running down the back of the inside of my coat.

My head was busted and the cold had slowed the bleeding down, but it was coming out now. "What happened?!" he yelled again. I was trying to tell him, but fear had engulfed me so, that all I could do was to sound like I had a bad case of asthma.

My sister began to tell him what had happened. He grabbed me up fast, and we were off to the hospital.

I had a hole in my head that required stitches, and dad was mad, but this time not at me. He was mad at the kids across the street for playing so rough.

He demanded that we not play with them anymore, because they might hurt one of us worse the next time. They were good kids, it was an accident and we got along great and had lots of fun, but now we were told we could not ever play with them again.

Of course as kids, we were not mad at each other, so we hid and played together anyway, until we got caught and got a beaten.

6

After a while it seemed as though we became enemies. We started fighting often and it sparked our dads to argue almost every evening. The man across the street would stand in his yard and dad would stand in ours, shouting at each other. I was so scared seeing dad that mad. Some nights he would speed off, I thought maybe to cool off, but he would come back still mad.

On this particular night they were arguing heavy. We were all standing on the porch and mama kept trying to tell dad to let it go and come back in the house. Dad seemed like he was in a trance, with his right hand in his back pocket arguing up a storm. Their dad kept trying to get dad to step into the street, but he wouldn't.

Seemed like everybody on our porch was crying, but the kids across the street were laughing and calling dad a chicken, "You are a chick'en!, You are a chick'en!."

Suddenly something happened, and the man started walking toward dad. Dad pulled his hand out of his back pocket and… pop!…pop!…pop! The man started scratching at his chest and ran back toward his house and fell at his doorstep.

It was like a nightmarish quietness…and it seemed like things started moving slow. Dad turned and started walking back toward us, taking long hurried but slow-motion steps. He walked between us through the front door and out the back door without looking at any of us, almost like he was in a trance.

Seemed like we were all frozen, the whole world seemed frozen. Then the kids across the street started crying.

Mom pulled us back in the house and it seemed like an eternity but the police pulled up in front of our house, with my dad in the backseat.

They took dad to jail that night and he was out the next day. We moved, never ever hearing anything about that incident, except later when dad would threaten us all by reminding us of that incident.

WOODS AND DIRT ROADS

When we left Bemis, we moved way out into the woods. An old house my mom use to live in. It was real scary at first, but we got use to it after a while.

We killed many snakes, mice and lots of bugs. We swung on grapevines and went on adventure trails and everything. We, the boys, were having the time of our lives.

We had to walk a ways to catch the bus, because it didn't come to our house. By that time, because of the move, we had transferred back to the school I started first grade in; Rosenwald.

I was going into the fifth grade by now, and this time around it was worse than at the "white" school. Kids were cruel, and because I was not able to fight back, I was an easy target; I got picked on a lot.

At the home front, we had hogs and a cow, which was my first real taste of "Country life". Something that had to be fed was an interesting concept.

This was also the place where we got a lot of beatings, and I don't remember a lot of what we did wrong, just seemed like dad was always mad. There were times we had to strip to get a beating, because" clothes cost too much to beat", dad would say.

I do recall a time when dad was about to take us to school because it was way too cold to walk to the bus stop that morning. We were in the cab of his truck and he was away from the truck a ways. He seemed to be doing something and saying something looking in our direction.

Johney and I jumped out of the truck and while I was trying to ask if he had called us, Johney beat me to it and asked, "did you call us?' By that time mom came out of the house and was standing on the porch.

"Did I call y'all?!" dad yelled, and picked up a brick or something and hurled it at us. He missed Johney by inches. Needless to say, fear engulfed me and I ran. I ran and jumped on the porch so fast, I don't think my feet touched the ground.

"Get over here and help me move this thing." It was something he wanted loaded on the truck or something, I don't even remember. I do, however, remember when we bent down to pick up that thing, while we were still in the bent position, he looked over at me and said "You know if I had hit Johney, I would have picked up something and knocked you out too?" I was terrified….. what a way to start out a school day.

We had no running water and an outhouse to use for our toilet. We had a creek we used the water from to take a bath and to wash clothes. I guess we didn't think much of it, it seemed like just the way life was suppose to be.

We had two potbellied stoves for heat in the winter and window fans in the summer. We stayed warm and cool and we ate well.

It seemed like mom and dad fought often, or dad fought mom, not just arguing but fighting. Every time he fought her, I would get even more afraid that some day he was going to kill her and us. He seemed to be angry most of the time.

We lived "smack dab" in the woods for about 2 years and befriended 2 white guys down the road who are friends until this day.

Chapter 2

GROWING UP

MEDON, TENNESSEE

During those 2 years in the "woods", dad was getting us a house built and we all were very excited about having running water and an indoor toilet and separate rooms from the girls.

We moved before I started 7th grade, and I was fascinated with the house. It seemed like we had really made it. Our water bill had to be high that first month, because I spent extra time flushing the toilet watching the water go down.

It was a treat just to walk to the edge of the driveway to catch the school bus, and we didn't have to get in coal or wood, because we had a floor furnace that heated the entire house. No more hauling water or heating water on the stove to take a bath.

However, we traded all that in for other chores. We had more room for more hogs, and chickens and fields to plant stuff in and to hoe and to pick stuff from. Dad called it a "truck patch." I didn't really know what that meant, but they were fields to us. Long rows for us to plant, hoe and pick! All the stuff we planted, hoed and picked, we survived off of. Mama would can and freeze a lot, so we ate well.

We had our own eggs, chickens and pork. We had to pick the coldest day of the year to kill hogs. It was completely bizarre our first hog killing day. My brothers and I had raised them from little pigs, and they were like pets to us. These men came in and killed our pets and we had to help with all that process, it was really bizarre. Needless to say we forgot about the bizarreness of it all when we had bacon for breakfast and fried pork chops for dinner.

It was here in this house where I got most of my beatings. Dad had a razor strap that he must have gotten from a barbershop somewhere. It was about three inches wide and about a foot and a half long, and about a half an inch thick.

Sometimes he wouldn't look for the razor strap, he would take off his belt, or make us go to the woods to get our own switches that he would plait together.

I remember once, we, my brother and I, were working with him in the back yard on something and he sent us to go get him a "pipe wrench" a tool we had always called a "monkey wrench." We looked vehemently for something that we thought might be it and although I had the "monkey wrench" in my hand, because I was unsure.

We were digging in a big tool box he had in the back of his truck when he came stomping around to the back of it, "is this it?" I asked, holding the wrench out to him. "Oh you'll know next time!" he said.

He snatched both of us out of the back of the truck, basically dragged us through the carport and threw us in the utility room. I have no idea where or when he pick up a hosepipe, but he retrieved one from somewhere and put our heads between his knees and wore our backsides out. After about three swats, I couldn't feel anything from the waist down, and could barely stand much less walk when it was all over.

HIGH SCHOOL

High school for me had its ups and downs. On one hand, it got me away from home but on the other it was "out of the frying pan into the fire."

Everybody seemed bigger, stronger and faster than I was, and since I had no athletic ability, I would get attention by being funny, and trying to be as cool as I could.

I was mostly easy going and happy-go-lucky, it took a lot to anger me, and when I was angered, I was too afraid to do anything about it.

Because I was so afraid of my dad, I felt very insecure in my ability to defend myself when it came to fighting, so I would try hard to avoid them. I would walk away, or play it off like it was no big deal, but deep down my feelings would hurt easily. I cried a lot, most of the time when nobody was watching.

I hated that I was so sensitive and tried hard not to let things bother me, but they did. No one told us back then about puberty, at least they didn't tell me. I had it bad, nose was too big, teeth were bucked, lips looked liked the guy on the Cosby Kids..... "Hey Hey Hey"!!

Thank God for hot combs, because I was at least able to have an afro to keep me feeling halfway decent about myself. Until dad decided to make us look "civilized" and cut it all off. I hated to go to school when that happened, because all the guys that picked on me anyway, had something else to make fun of.

Since I was so skinny, my clothes wouldn't fit right, so I was always afraid to take off my jacket, even in the summer time. I would try to wear some kind of jacket to hide my frame.

The girls seemed to always like me, I guess because I was funny and made them laugh, but it was never enough to have a relationship. I use to tell a joke about the fact that there was only one pretty girl in my whole high school, and she could bench press a cow.

Most of the girls were in awe of the basketball players or guys who had their own cars or were just cool, way cooler than I was. I was just funny.

I played trumpet in 10th 11th and 12th grade and finally felt like I was doing something in high school that I could be proud of.

I remember trying to learn how to smoke in the band equipment room; what a site. I had been getting cigarettes from this guy and really thought I was smoking; when I found out that you are suppose to inhale the smoke! I was just sucking it in and blowing it out. On that particular day the equipment room was full of people, girls and all. I took a big draw and inhaled it!...... it felt like I had inhaled a car! I thought my chest was going to explode and I couldn't breathe! I started passing gas and everything! I could see, because I couldn't hear anything, people falling all over everything laughing. When I finally could breathe and cleaned my nose and got up off the floor, all I could do was laugh as well. Needless to say I found out that smoking would never be my thing.

I really enjoyed band, the parades and the band trips were awesome, when we were allowed to go. A lot of the times I was too afraid to ask dad anything about outside activities, I never knew how he was going to respond. My older sister played the clarinet and my brother played the drums. I remember when each of us first brought our instruments home to practice, we were horrible, but each of us learned to play our instruments quite well.

I had a couple of really good friends, we understood each other and were closer than most. We laughed a lot, which got us in trouble a lot as well.

I had my first real sexual encounter on prom night and I was hooked!!!

I made a lot of really good friends in high school, girls and guys, but never really kept up with any after graduation.

Sometime before graduation I went to test for the Marines, I really didn't know what I wanted to do after high school so I thought that the Armed Forces would be a great place to start.

I remember catching the bus to Memphis, Tennessee and staying at the Peabody Hotel. They feed us breakfast and it was off to the testing.

Sometime during one of the breaks I got scared. Most of the guys were bigger than I was and was telling me that guys my size never made it through boot camp…..it scared me to death!

I went back in and just started marking things, I didn't even read the questions, I just marked answers.

Needless to say, I didn't pass the exam so I proved unqualified to join the Marines. I thought they would never leave me alone after that. They called often until I graduated to reschedule for the test, but my mind was made up not to join the Armed Forces.

I graduated high school from West Sr. High in Denmark, Tennessee in 1975. There were about 73 of us that year and I was glad to get out. Not only out of high school, but away from home as well. I felt like I was finally free and rid of all that fear.

Chapter 3

THE AWAKENING

FLINT, MICHIGAN

I had been accepted to Tennessee State University in Nashville as an Art Education major before graduation, but I was so ready to leave I didn't want to stay home until August so I went to Flint, Michigan to stay with relatives.

Feeling like a caged animal being set free in the wild, it was "no holds barred" for me until August. I smoked as much pot and drank as much alcohol as I could stomach, not realizing at the time it was to mask and numb all the pain and insecurities I had encountered up to that point.

I didn't know what it felt like not to be afraid and terrified every waking moment of the day. This was a welcomed experience and I wanted more.

My cousins seemed so much more advanced than I. I felt like a "dumb ole hillbilly" trying to fit in with the fast pace lifestyle of my "city folk" cousins.

I managed somehow to make it through that summer, make a few new friends and was the butt of a few jokes. That was how it was with me I guess, if you can't keep up, "make 'em laugh."

It was in Flint that I realized that I hated my upbringing and the way I felt about myself. How I had allowed people to push me around and not fight back. Trying to hide it behind laughter was beginning to wear thin.

Anger was beginning to build up inside me and a spirit of revenge was starting to manifest itself and I had no idea how to handle it.

TENNESSEE STATE UNIVERSARY

It was August of 1975 when I settled in at TSU. I seemed like an insect among giants. I had never been around that many people at one time in my life.

Girls! All shapes and sizes, shades and colors, the likes that I had never experienced. I went from a few decent girls in high school, to a smorgasbord of all kinds.

With that many girls, seemed like all I had to do was to throw my line out and some of them would bite, so I did, and they did. It was all about me in college, I was not really concerned about anybody's feelings except mine. I tried to "date" as many girls as I could juggle without them finding out about each other. Especially now that I realized I wasn't half bad after all. It seemed like I was being driven by a force to conquer, whatever that meant.

I started boxing, took Judo and studied as much on self-discipline as I could; basically trying to control the hostility that I knew was inside me. I tried hard to avoid arguing and raising my voice in a discussion. I was a great fan of Star Trek's "Mr. Spock" I thought he was the coolest guy in the world when it came to discipline. However, I wanted to know I could take care of myself if needed, and to feel confident enough to protect my mom if she ever reported to me that my dad had hurt her in any way.

College life was slightly awkward for me. I majored in Art Education the first year because I loved to draw; however being graded and critiqued and micro observed was not something I had expected. I soon became disinterested with drawing altogether, totally distant from how I at one time felt. It just wasn't for me, so I didn't take it serious. I tell people today, I majored in Frat Parties and girls and made a 4.0 in Living Single.

I would go back and forward to Michigan during breaks and eventually changed my College Major to Communications Speech and Drama.

It was during this time when it seemed like something happened inside me that took me to an area that I called the "dark side." I was almost normal in the daytime, but a complete criminal at night. Robbing, stealing and manipulating the places I worked in to find ways to spy out their vulnerabilities to take ultimate advantage of them. The Love of money became an all out real obsession for me, and getting it anyway I could, seemed almost normal.

LIVING A DOUBLE LIFE

By 1977 I had officially become a resident of Nashville TN. I was a full time Karate student, had a part time job, and hitting and missing in college. Not to mention I had a son born that July. Needless to say, my priorities were way off.

I wanted to make sure I always had money so I did whatever I had to do to get it. Most of the people I was around had no idea of the double life I was living,

I learned to conceal it well. Even when I was arrested for an attempted theft, I had a mug shot and fingerprint done, but the charges were dropped, and I kept on moving. It was like a drive to mischief when the sun went down. It seemed as though I was overtaken with something when it came to getting what I wanted. I learned to talk women out of almost anything, and could seem to sense vulnerable opportunities. I seemed to not feel or care about hurting people's feelings to obtain my warped desires.

Somehow I was still managing to stay in school and became very familiar with a Richard Pryor's monologue and performed it on a college talent show one night and brought the house down. Coming off stage a guy grabbed me by the arm and said "man you can get booked with that act in Vegas." Wow! That was the spring board that launched my short comedy career, and I was off to the races. I was trying to turn over every stone of opportunity I could to try to get it off the ground.

Still battling with my "demons," I tried hard to focus on positive things but still found myself being pulled back to the streets. Engaging in criminal activities seemed to not be what I wanted to do, but it was a constant fight to stay normal.

Living a double life became more and more difficult as I tried to transcend from criminality to normality.

MY "BIG" BREAK

Speaking in front of people had always been a challenge for me because of my stuttering problem, but once I got started and got my first laugh I was okay. What made it even easier was that I was using Richard Pryor's voice and material.

It was the summer of 1979; I had pulled an armed robbery and got only 13 dollars. That helped me to make my mind up that that was it, time to focus on the comedy thing, since it seemed to be working for me. I had made friends with a popular DJ at the radio station and he got me an audition for "writer's night" at the Exit Inn in Nashville. He told me that I had to do my own material because it was for original artists only. That terrified me, because I had never performed anything of my own before, but I showed up anyway like I had it all together.

I had an old guitar I took with me that I played around with doing Elvis impressions. I had no idea what I was going to do, but as I sat and watched the other acts, mostly singing, I came up with my act; a little Elvis, a little talking and for the finale "Super Dude" an episode in the life of Superman, if he were Black.

It worked! I was booked for my first paid job as a standup! I was to be the opening act for Norman Conners, a famous Jazz artist I had never heard of, but he was coming that September for 2 nights.

I was blown away and terrified because I had no idea what all that meant. I learned a lot from that experience and it started me on a 5 year journey of opening up for well-known artists of that time.

Being a Black comedian in Country Music City USA made it very difficult to get an agent, so I did all my own bookings and negotiations.

I performed in The Tennessee Theater in Nashville, The Hyde- A- Way Club and a new night club opened up that gave me regular work called the Byrd's Nest, it was owned by Bobby Byrd, a former member of James Brown's "Famous Flames."

Some of the groups I opened for were; The Staple Singers, Stacey Lattimore, Candi Staton, The Chi Lites, Harold Melvin and the Blue Notes, The Manhattans, Ray, Goodman and Brown, Eddie Kendricks, Bobby Blue Bland, and Jerry Butler to name a few.

It was during my opening for the Manhattans when I met Deborah whom I think I fell in love with at first sight. I had never really had any problems with obtaining female companionship at any given night after my performances, and this night was no different. A lady walked up to me and said that someone would like to meet me, so I followed her and she introduced me to Deborah Wilson, even though it was slightly dark and smoky, something about her struck my heart.

There were 3 kinds of women I usually tried to avoid; women with ex-husbands, baby daddies and women with a cigarette habit, I would later find out that Deborah fit all those slots, but my heart fell for her and so did I.

Chapter 4

REAPING THE CONSEQUENCES

THE ARREST

Deborah and I started dating in about April 1980, and I had never witnessed anyone laughing as hard as she did. It seemed like she was free for the first time, and it felt good knowing that she was loving being around me.

I never mentioned to her about my past, because I felt like it was all over and I had turned over a new leaf. This comedy thing was going to really do it for me.

I worked in a shoe store in the mall by this time and was trying to put my past behind me. I was still fighting in karate tournaments and doing standup when the opportunities presented themselves.

One particular off day, I was going to pick Deborah up for lunch in downtown Nashville where she worked as I had done at other times. I knew my tags had expired, but I had intended to pick them up the following week, so when the police stopped me I thought nothing of it except get a ticket, get my tags, go to court and get it dismissed.

Needless to say everything went totally to the left! Policemen start coming in from everywhere! I saw through my rearview window, to the right and left of my car in front and seemed like from the sky. I saw through my side mirror the policeman that stopped me approaching my car with his hand on his revolver, "Step out of the car please, we have a year and a half old warrant for your arrest!" It seemed like things started moving in slow motion as he handcuffed me, put me in the back seat of the squad car and headed me off to jail.

Once we were at the booking station they had that previous mug shot that the victim had supposedly picked out. They had the date the place and the license number of my vehicle, an open and shut case, but I denied everything.

Things were going so good for me and people had such an image of me, I couldn't admit to something of that magnitude. It was a shameful thing and I wanted no parts of it. The way I was perceived by my peers and the public made it extremely difficult to confess to such an uncharacteristic act.

I spent 3 days in jail and a policeman friend that Deborah knew, came and got me out on my own recognizance, that I would show up for the Preliminary Hearing, the hearing that would determine whether it was worth the court pursuing.

The Preliminary Hearing was set for the following week and Deborah came to court with me. I was terrified because I didn't know what would happen. I had slightly remembered that one and I didn't know whether anyone would remember what I looked liked. I was just hoping that because I looked completely different than the mug shot, and the way I looked a year and a half ago, that they would not know me.

Deborah and I were sitting in the court room on the end of one of the benches when my Public Defender, the Prosecutor, this woman and a man came up to us and was asked if I was the one who robbed her. She looked familiar to me but I couldn't tell. She looked at me and they all walked away. Deborah started crying in disbelief that they handled it that way and I was in shock that there was no line up, because there had been no positive identification up to that point. My mug shot had been chosen with two others the night of the robbery.

The Public Defender came back to us and said "she said his glasses and hair are different but that's him." With all that, I still couldn't admit to the crime or any affiliation to any criminal activity anywhere at any time. I was stuck in denial mode and had convinced myself that they had the wrong man and somehow I was going to get off.

STILL PURSUING THE DREAM

I guess I was so convinced in my mind that somehow this would all go away; I kept pursuing the comedy dream. Opportunities were coming and I was enjoying the ride. It was really awesome what they paid me for what I did, and all I could see was bigger and better. I knew I would eventually have to leave Nashville if I really wanted to "make it big." I felt like I had what it took to succeed in that arena.

It seemed like all was happening was a constant continuation of court dates, I would show up for one thing or another but it didn't seem like my case was that important to anyone, even the Prosecutors.

I eventually lost my job at the shoe store because they had a shakedown of sorts and because of what I was going through in court and the fact that I had not put down my first arrest I was the prime target to be released.

Becoming a small time celebrity in hot pursuit of a big dream made it even more difficult to face up to something as demeaning as an armed robbery, especially when everyone else thought you were innocent.

The Municipal Auditorium, The Tennessee Theatre and a few local television programs allowed me more opportunities to perform and it took me deeper into denial mode. I had prominent individuals believing in me and I didn't have the heart to let then in on my criminal past, and besides, sometimes court appearances were so far and in between I just knew they were going to dismiss everything.

Although I was still a nervous wreck standing in front of people, somehow I made it work. It didn't seem like nothing was slowing me down so I kept moving forward trying in every way to get discovered even in Nashville, Country Music City USA.

MARRIAGE AND FAMILY

Deborah and I decided to get married January 1, 1982. She had no idea of the truth and I was so convinced that it was all going to disappear somehow, I didn't bother to tell her.

Almost 3 years after the crime and about a year and a few months since the arrest. By this time I had a paid attorney and it still looked like nothing was happening in court.

I had started working at a service station and we moved into an apartment on the west side of Nashville. Things couldn't have been better or happier for me. I was with the woman I loved, a daughter and my son from Michigan who would come down to visit at times.

Life seemed to be coming together for me and it seemed like the past was a very distant galaxy away. I was still competing in karate tournaments and still doing standup when the occasion arose.

Deborah and I partied a lot but we took care of business. I felt uneasiness in the fact that she made really good money and I had steady work and an occasional gig, but still didn't feel like I was contributing as much as I would have liked.

Feeling a sense of lacking I figure out as I had done in the past, a way to steal money from the place I worked until I slipped up and was caught and fired. What in the world is wrong with me? How come I couldn't leave well enough alone? Nobody seemed to care about the money issue except me. Why couldn't I just leave well enough alone, enjoy my family, work, do my karate and my gigs and be happy? What a blow, but it was my own fault, still I made it seem as though I had been set up because they found out about me awaiting trial.

TRIAL AND VERDICT

January 1, 1983, marked one year of being married, almost 4 years from the crime. I was working at a grocery store by this time and still moving forward. Then I got the call that a trial date had been set for January 26. For some reason I was pretty confident that things were going to go in my favor. We had tried unsuccessfully to combat the lie that was told by the victim, her dad, my public defender and the prosecutor at that time concerning how they set me up at the identification procedure. Now the moment of truth had come and we were headed to trial.

Deborah and I went to see the Attorneys about a week before and the prosecutors had made me an offer of five years. I had no idea what that meant, armed robbery carried 10 to life so I could get 10 years or more or do five or take it to trial and get off completely. My attorneys were confident that a jury would not find me guilty and I had a better chance of getting off than getting convicted. They even said, "That's not a deal," so I turned down the deal and went to trial.

I thought I had everything in my favor, I had an old girlfriend that was suppose to say I was with her in Alabama at the time of the robbery, who clammed up and shut down on the witness stand. All the character witnesses I had were not allowed to testify. It was a long day of nothing going in my favor. It was like a preplanned circus and I was the clown. Even when I testified, it was like just another part of the circus that nobody believed.

The trial started at 9am and it was almost midnight before closing arguments and jury deliberation. I was really nervous by this time and we were instructed not to leave the building on top of that. It really hit me then, they could give me anywhere from 10 years to life for 13 dollars.

It seemed like a lifetime but it was about an hour when the jury came back in. The bailiff found us in the cafeteria, where I really couldn't eat anyway, and told us. We went back into the courtroom and it seemed like I was a dead man walking. I was numb all over and seemed like I was in a cave of some sorts, as my attorneys motioned me to come to the table.

"Will the defendant please rise, has the jury reached its verdict?" "Yes your honor, we the jury find the defendant Anthony Walton GUILTY of robbery with the use of a deadly weapon." I looked over at Deborah with a glazed look and was about to pass out when I grabbed some water to compose myself. "We impose the sentence in the amount of 12 years in the State Penitentiary."

I did the best I could to hold myself up when they handcuffed me and walked me out, Deborah was crying, but trying to control herself, and held on to me hard when they allowed us to embrace in the hallway.

What had I done? How did I get her involved in all this? Oh my! This was not expected, not now, not tonight. The thought of her driving home this time of night in her condition caused such a helpless feeling in the pit of my stomach.

Being taken to the jail that night was like a death march and I was being taken to my doom. It was like the world had stopped to a slow crawl and I had no control whatsoever. All I could think about is what have I done?

MAKING BOND AND MAKING CHANGES

Because of the date of the crime, my charge and sentence was under a different law which afforded me an opportunity to make bond to work on my Appeal, and possibly reverse the verdict. I was in jail for a few days and Deborah's grandmother agreed to put her house up for a bond for me to be released.

Now I was really trapped, found guilty for something that everybody thought I was innocent of when I knew better, but was somehow still convinced that I could beat it. Even if I confessed to it now, what would it benefit, so I felt I had to play it out.

We had to move in with Deborah's grandmother to try to save money for the lawyers to file the appeal. Life was getting more and more complicated by now and I didn't know how to handle it. I still had my job, so at least I was working and still able to contribute while waiting for calls to perform.

I felt like I was being watched, so I straightened up considerably hoping that they, whoever they were would somehow see that I really wasn't a bad guy. For the past 5 years I had really made some drastic changes in my life and it seemed like hopefully that would count for something.

Not really understanding the law, I had hoped that all that time passed and my little celebrity status would make some kind of a difference. I also had hopes that somehow the issues I brought up on Appeal would be enough to overturn the conviction.

In the meantime we moved in with Deborah's brother, who had just purchased a home, and it made it perfect for our family as well. Life was continuing to move but there was always in the back of my mind, "what if" what if I had to go do 12 years? What if I lost my family completely?

WEEKS AND MONTHS GOING BY

Every now and then I was terrified at the thought of going to prison, but when an opportunity to perform or a karate tournament would come up, I would be ok. I didn't say much to anyone about my anxieties cause it seemed like everyone else was going on with living and not worrying about me having to go to prison, they felt like justice would prevail, yet I was hoping that it wouldn't.

Every special occasion, like birthdays and holidays, made me wonder if I would be there for the next one which made it very difficult to enjoy them. Deborah and I tried to live as normal as possible, still clubbing and partying like there was no tomorrow. I kept thinking in my mind that all this was eventually going to go away and there would never be a need to reveal to anyone that side of me and the life I had lived before.

Weeks and months had gone by and nothing, the lawyers were saying that no news is good news, but it takes a while to complete those Appeals. I was losing myself, but I couldn't share with anyone what I was feeling. By this time and the distance I had come from the person I use to be, I had almost convinced myself that they had the wrong man and that a grave injustice had been carried out.

Although Deborah and I were uncertain about everything, we didn't talk much about it, as a matter of fact, we almost grew apart. I guess the pressure from everything was too much for us to comprehend and since we didn't know how to handle it, we just went through the motions.

Christmas of 1983 was a blur and so was our 2nd year Wedding Anniversary Celebration in January 1984. Although I knew that the courts closed down for the holidays, I still had no idea what to expect. I just wanted to crawl in a hole and die or somehow make all this anticipation go away.

Sometime toward the middle of January, I got myself an engagement at a new comedy club in Nashville called Zanies and I felt good about that. This was what I felt like I needed to give myself a new start on my career, if maybe I could get past this court thing.

Chapter 5

NO LAUGHING MATTER

ZANIES

It was the third week of February 1984, I had finished what I felt was my biggest comedy night ever. As I walked off stage a lady grabbed my hand, stuck a card in it and said, "Call me, I think I can help you." There were so many people grabbing me and shaking my hand, I didn't see her I just heard her voice.

I do, however, remember some guy stopped me, very offended at something I had said, and threatened me. I got so mad, I wanted to hit him but I didn't, I just threatened him back and walked off.

Later I was ashamed of myself for losing my cool. I had been proud for still being able to be funny and in control in the midst of waiting for the outcome of my future. To observe me performing, you would have never known I had been convicted of armed robbery, waiting on the Court of Appeals to hear my case and overturn the verdict.

It had been a little over a year since the trial, and almost 5 years since the crime. I'd hoped that everything was going to be all right, so I went on doing stand up comedy, waiting on my big break. The lady who grabbed my hand just happen to be a talent agent from Music Row, this was my night! She was very impressed with my style of comedy and was ready to start bookings. I was so excited; I didn't know what to do. After a little over 3 years of performing, my break had finally come.

THE WORST NEWS IN THE WORLD

Feeling good about a new start-up on the comedy venture was short lived when I received the call I had dreaded; I was at work the morning the call came in from my attorney.

"Anthony?" he said

"Yes!" I replied.

"We just received the letter for you to surrender custody." He said.

"Huh?" I said.

"The letter came in today for you to surrender custody." He stated again.

"What do you mean surrender custody?" I asked, knowing what it meant, but hoping it didn't.

"You've got to turn yourself in on March 7th, 1984 at the Sheriff's Department; the Court of Appeals upheld the verdict." He explained.

"Did they reduce it or anything?" I asked.

"No" he responded.

I couldn't believe it! My heart almost stopped beating, my head started spinning out of control, my knees buckled, and I sat down on some bales of sacks by the phone. My mouth open, the phone fell to the floor, sweat poured out like water, my breathing was shallow, and I know I looked like I had seen a ghost. I felt like I was in a tunnel and the rest of the world was out of my reach. This was the worst news I had ever heard in my life; they gave me a week to start my 12-year sentence in prison.

The Manager of the store saw me and must have known what had happened because he told me to just go home. I didn't live far from the store but the drive seemed like it took forever.

My thoughts went to Deborah. How was I going to tell my wife? We had sincerely believed that it wouldn't come to this and now here it was. She'll need to go ahead and file for a divorce, because surely this marriage couldn't last. It will be better for both of us if she were free. We'd only been married for 2 years and had only known each other for a little less than 4 years. The marriage was not strong enough to last through a 12-year prison sentence, under any circumstances, much less these.

TELLING DEBORAH, IT'S OVER

I was sick inside, my stomach was in knots but I couldn't loose control, I had to be strong and unemotional. I had to be strong to keep Deborah strong. The only reasonable thing to do was to tell her what the Lawyer had said, and then tell her what she needed to do, file for a divorce.

I sat at home waiting for her to get off work, trying to determine how to tell her that the appeal had been denied, and I was supposed to surrender custody March 7th, but there was no way I could tell her easy, nothing was coming to mind. I didn't know what her reaction might be but I knew I had to be in control. I tried to prepare myself for whatever she might say or do. I felt like she would say that she wanted to stay with me and wait until I got out, but I knew in my heart that she wouldn't, the relationship just wasn't close enough. My head was hurting, and my heart was melting. My marriage, my career, my life was ending, and there was nothing I could do about it. It seemed so unfair; I ached all over!

We had lived that year like we knew I wouldn't have to go to prison. We didn't spend much time together; we took one another for granted. We went out without each other and spent very little time relating to one another. Then I started to realize how very important she was to me, but it was too late now. In my heart I felt like it wouldn't last, it was over!

I waited for her to come home and a numb feeling was over me as she walked in the door. I looked at her as if I would never see her again. We did our usual greetings but this time she knew something was wrong. I was holding her tightly, "what's wrong?" she asked. "The Lawyer called, I. I've got to turn myself in on March 7th" I replied. She started crying and asking me a lot of questions I couldn't answer. She cried most of the night asking, "Why is this happening to us? What did we do to deserve this?" I felt terrible, my wife is crying, normally I could comfort her, but this time there was no comfort. I didn't know what to do or say, I just tried to keep myself from breaking up. The pain was almost unbearable, so many thoughts running through my head, what's going to happen, to her, to my daughter, to my life?

THE LAST DAYS OF FREEDOM AND
SURRENDERING CUSTODY

The last few days were very strange; it was like we were trying to make up for the year that we lost not loving or showing love to each other. We were like glue day and night, she never said anything about divorce, but seemed more determined to stay and fight for my freedom.

March 7th, 1984, my mom came down from Jackson, TN and my sisters went to the Sheriff's Department with me. Everybody was like zombies nobody said anything. When they came up and got me I hugged everyone with a slight smile, trying to assure them I was okay, but I really wasn't. I hugged Deborah last; we just held each other and seemed to let go just before the emotions fell. She appeared strong and determined, but I could see the hurt.

I turned and went in with the guard. It was a long walk, seemed underground, no windows and slightly dim. The guard was an older man, about 55, a little bigger than I was and very fragile looking. Years of experience in karate and tournaments had given me a lot of confidence in my ability to handle myself, so I thought about taking his gun and his clothes and walking out. He made himself so vulnerable; he walked slightly in front of me, slightly peering at me from the corner of his eyes. The gun was directly in front of my left hand…then what? What would I do? I couldn't go back home, life could never be the way I wanted it.

I could never be able to pursue my career, I couldn't live life on the run, and it would never work. So I erased the thought and went humbly along.

THE HOLDING TANK

I was placed in a holding tank with another guy for about 2 hours. They had taken my watch, my wedding band and my clothes. My wedding band had not been off since the day I married. When I had to take it off it felt like my heart came out with it. I hadn't realized what it had meant; my marriage was my life source. I had just realized how much I needed my wife and my daughter. I sat in the holding tank emotionless just staring straight ahead. The other guy was talking to me but I never responded to anything, I just stared ahead. Thousands of thoughts were going through my head; I went over my life and wondered how it could have ended up like this.

Later they came and got me and put me in a cell with three guys. The cell was only big enough for one person. I was able to touch both walls with my hands out to the side of me. I slept that night stooped in a corner by the commode. I felt like an animal packed in a cage. The pain from the thoughts of 12 years and the smell made me sick. I either passed out or went hard to sleep, missing my wife terribly.

IT'S REALLY HAPPENING

I awakened the next morning hoping that it all had been a bad dream but realizing how real it was. I kept feeling like something was going to happen; that they would change their minds and realize I didn't need to be in here.

Because of my charges they moved me up to the 5th floor, where all the violent offenders were. The murderers, rapists, armed robbers and all other violent inmates were on this floor. I don't belong here, I kept thinking. Even the guards seemed a little hesitant about putting me in with inmates that had violent charges. I stood out like a sore thumb. I guess I was hurting so badly I didn't think about being afraid.

How could things be this way? Just the other day people were cheering for me and making me feel like I was somebody; now I'm nothing but a violent criminal that needs to be off the street. I wanted to yell, but I knew I couldn't because it would show a sign of weakness and weak people got taken advantage of.

I talked to Deborah off and on and she was working so hard to get me out or something. I don't think either one of us knew what we were trying to do we just kept thinking that surely the system would realize that I didn't belong here. I kept thinking that maybe if we could get something done quickly then I wouldn't have to go to the main prison.

I looked around at the other inmates; they looked just like what television stereotyped them as, hard! They looked every bit like hardened criminals and it seemed as though most of them knew each other. At first they just kind of looked at me and I looked back at them. Later when we started talking one of them told me I looked like I wanted to hit somebody. They all seemed so relaxed and at home; seemed like they couldn't wait to get to the main prison and start doing some "real time"! I was hurting inside and just the thought of 12 years in prison made my stomach turn upside down.

Deborah came out to see me a couple of times and I would smile. The whole time she was there and having to talk to her through glass made it seem more barbaric and dehumanizing. We would say nice things to each other - things we hadn't said in years and that hurt. I kept thinking what does it matter now? What is it going to benefit now? Our life as we've known it is over. It is no use fooling ourselves...but I loved her so much, and she looked better to me then than ever before. I grew sicker as the days would increase.

Chapter 6

MY LOVE AND MY LIFE

DEBORAH

Deborah Wilson was her name when I met her. Her friends called her "Teenie" but I called her Deborah. We met in a nightclub after doing one of my stand-up routines. I didn't think much of her then because of her approach, but later grew to know her to be as sweet and pleasant as a morning in spring.

She was delightful and sexy and the harder I tried not to fall in love with her the more I did. I got to the point where I didn't want to be without her so on January 1, 1982 I married her. Our relationship blossomed like a rose; in the beginning we were very close.

She encouraged me to involve myself in my son Anthony's life, who was from a previous relationship, and lived in Flint, Mich.

Life was like a storybook for me until the conviction. After that it seemed as though the marriage took a turn. We didn't argue or fight, it just seemed like all the feelings and emotions in the relationship began to waiver.

We had to move out of our apartment. We moved in with her grandmother and later with her brother. I was feeling more helpless and dependent than I had ever felt in my adult life but I still tried to maintain my self-control and I still loved her deeply.

Now sitting in jail watching her come and go, being unable to touch her, caused sharp pains to shoot through my heart and head. I felt like I was going to explode.

We'd only been separated twice before but only for a couple of nights at a time in the four years that we had known each other. Once in October 1980 when I was arrested for the crime and later in January 1983 after the conviction.

I felt weak inside, all I could I think of was holding her and letting her know how much I loved her and wanted to take care of her. I didn't know whether that would ever be possible again.

JAIMEE

Jaimee was our daughter she was 10 years old about to turn 11. She was only 6 when I met them but we had a very real and natural relationship.

It seemed like some force was causing me to think about them so much especially at night. All I would do was think about how much I needed them and how much I loved them and longed to be with them as a husband and father.

I tried not to think about it because of the pain but there was no way I could get around it. At night when I slept, I dreamed about being out and happy but when I would awaken I'd realize I was locked up without them and deeply, very deeply unhappy. I would rather have been a free dog than a caged man.

I'M DYING SLOWLY INSIDE

This was not going to work and I had just begun the sentence. Let's be logical, I thought, I shouldn't expect Deborah to wait for me. She didn't do anything wrong, why should she have to suffer as well? I need to tell her or insist that she never come back, file for a divorce, and go on with her life, but I didn't have the guts. The thought of it ate through me like a cancer.

SHIPPING DAY

The day came when I was to be moved to the Reception Center, the place inmates went to be classified as to what prison they were going to be sent to. They gave me all of my personal belongings back including my ring. I clenched it fast in my fist and realized how much this little item meant. I was wondering how Deborah was doing and hoped she wasn't hurting as badly as I was.

Only about 6 of us went that day. It was horrifying as they chained us up together. They had chains on our hands, feet and waist and they walked us across the street with 2 or 3-armed guards. I felt my pride being stripped away like an old shirt. I walked at the end of those guys in total humiliation and shame. It was about 8:00 am, and a lot of people were on the streets. I just kept my head down in embarrassment while all the other guys were yelling at girls. They walked us to a van, loaded us up and left for the prison. In the back of the van, no one was saying anything. I kept looking at my chains and thought to myself, "it's over. There is no way out! Nobody can do anything to help, I'm in the mouth of the beast and there's nothing I can do about it".

My thoughts raced to Deborah and Jaimee, it's been 3 weeks since I've seen them and my soul yearned for that. Where am I going? What's going to happen to me? What's going to become of my family? I felt like the other guys in the van were thinking the same things but they appeared strong so I needed to be in control of myself. I kept thinking, how in the world could I have ended up like this? I had a very promising career, a job to keep money in my pockets and a beautiful family...all for what? Just to have my life ended chained up like a vicious criminal and stripped like a dog in the pound?

I looked out the window noticing everyone else in the world was going on with their lives, but for me, my life had ended. There was nothing else for me except prison for the next 12 years and there was no one to help.

THE SILENT SCREAM

I watched the road signs trying to get a feel of where I was. As we drove up to the prison and I saw the razor wire and barbed wire a wild panic came over me. I wanted to scream...NO!! I thought to myself, "I can't go in there, I don't belong in there!" I believe that if I hadn't been chained to the other guys as soon as the guard opened the door I would have leaped from the van and ran like a wild man.

We pulled inside the gate and I saw the gate close shut, I realized then I was no longer a part of the human race and that my life as I had known it had ended. A big lump swelled up in my throat. I tried to remain in control; it felt like a vice was squeezing my head.

Human beings, by changing the inner attitudes of their minds, can change the outer aspects of their lives.

William James (1842 - 1910)

Chapter 7

INTROSPECT AND RETROSPECT

THE VIEW FROM INSIDE

Inside the gates were about 15 buildings that looked like dorms or barracks except one place. It had been fenced off with razor and barbed wire; that's where our van stopped, a prison inside a prison.

As we were getting out of the van other inmates were shouting things at us. I didn't understand what they were saying I was just wishing for a way out and wishing I was home and that this was just a nightmare.

INTAKE

It was still before noon and they had taken off my regular clothes and had given me prison clothes to put on; a pair of jeans, a tee shirt, some boots and a jacket. When I put those clothes on I may as well have put on a ball and chain. I asked the officer "What will happen to my old clothes?" he said "What difference does it make, you belong to the State now Mister." He was reading my papers that came with me, "you've got 12 years, and these clothes should be the last thing you should be worrying about."

Twelve years I thought as they led me to an empty cell. The cells were bigger than the one downtown and the doors were made of wood. Twelve years is a long time I kept thinking. How can I do 12 years? They put me inside the cell, closed the door and locked it. When the door locked it felt like every bone in my body shook and all my strength left me. I stood there realizing that I had nothing and no one.

THE SENSE OF HOPELESSNESS AND DEATH

The sense of hopelessness and despair that I felt at that time is indescribable. My head was about to explode, my eyes filled up with water, my knees buckled as I backed up to the bunk. The covers were folded up in a pile and I took the sheet and started wiping my eyes. I couldn't think of myself spending days and nights like this for 12 years; the thought was sickening.

I sat, seemingly for hours. Darkness was beginning to settle in and I was wondering what Deborah and Jaimee were doing about this time and what we would be doing if I were there. They brought a dinner plate and sat it on the bunk I didn't move, I didn't even know if I was breathing; I really wanted to die.

As darkness fell outside, it was falling on the inside for me. My life was meaningless and dark; there was no hope and no reason to live. I couldn't bear knowing that my wife would leave me and become another man's wife while my life rotted away in a hellhole.

THERE'S ONLY ONE WAY OUT

Why didn't I plead guilty? Why did they wait so long to send me here? Why now? I'm not a dangerous criminal? I don't belong in prison, not now! I can't do it; I'm not going to do it. It was all clear to me; death was the only way out!

The sheet I was wiping my eyes with earlier was still in my hands and immediately I started unfolding it and twisting it up to make it more like a rope. It was like I was in a trance; I couldn't see beyond those prison walls. I couldn't bear the pain; I wanted to stop the pains of loneliness and despair; the head that hurt from strained emotional pressure; the eyes that were swollen from strained tears. I sat twisting the sheet realizing the only way I could stop the pain was death. The depth and the severity of the pain and anger I was feeling can't be described by words.

The more I thought about what had happened to me the more I hurt with anger. The more I thought about my family the more I hurt with loneliness. My heart was pounding as though it was going to explode. Flashes of my life, my wife, my daughter were racing through my head…I can't handle it, I just can't, I've got to end this now.

I looked up, studying the pipes that ran through my room trying to decide which one would hold me up. It sounded like drums were pounding as my heart was beating through my chest. My breathing was becoming very shallow almost non-existing. I searched the cell desperately looking for what I felt would be a strong enough pipe because I wanted to do it right. As I looked toward the back of the cell toward the window my eyes focused down. In the corner of the window there was a Bible, old and the back torn off, but I knew it was a Bible.

Chapter 8

MY PERSONAL TESTIMONY

A RAY OF HOPE SHINES THROUGH

It appeared as though time stopped and everything got quiet. I glared at the Bible like a curious animal after hearing a strange sound. It felt as though I was coming out of a deep trance and life was beginning to return. I hadn't thought about praying or anything, I just wanted out of this pain. Seeing the Bible seemed to have weakened the force that was driving me to end my life. I thought to myself if there is a God would He hear me? Would He even care?

I started remembering Sunday school and how the teacher would always tell me that Jesus cares, He loves even the worst sinner. I knew I wasn't the worst sinner but I was a sinner and I felt like I didn't have a right to ask for help but I did anyway. I laid down the sheet and got on my knees beside the bed, clenched my hands together and prayed, as a matter of fact, I begged!

THE PRAYER FOR HELP

Please God help me, I don't want to die but I don't want to live like this either. Help me; I'm hurting so badly I can't stand it. I've lost everything, I have nothing and I am nothing. I'm helpless and I have no hope for tomorrow. God I love my family and I can't stand the loneliness, my head hurts and my heart aches from brokenness; If you don't help me there is no help for me.

A SIGN FROM GOD

My heart emptied out as I prayed and told God all about my hurts and fears and I felt as though He was standing beside my bed. It had been raining, thundering and lightening and it stopped and gave me a sense of peace. For the first time since the conviction I had a sense of hope that this was not the end and that there was a God who was able to help. I got the Bible from the window and dusted it off. I felt like it had been my lifesaver, for had it not been in the window my life would have ended that night.

I slept in peace and with the feeling of confidence that everything was going to work out fine and sometime during the night I gained strength to face tomorrow. I had waken up with my wife for two years and I couldn't keep her out of my mind but I awoke the next day with a new hold on life and a determination to survive.

Chapter 9

MIXED EMOTIONS

THE JOURNEY BEGINS

I was in that particular building for a few days without anyone talking to me about my time or where I was going from there. I was very lost and confused. I was waiting for Saturday to come so that I could see Deborah. I was excited, nervous and hurting all at the same time. I wanted to see her but I didn't, I hadn't held her in my arms in at least a month and I didn't know how I was going to react. I felt emotionally drained and weak, just knowing that I would see her and hold her in my arms again. I was held in "intake" where all new inmates stay until bed space is available. We were only allowed to go outside for 1 hour a day and 23 hours in the cell. I had no radio or TV so I spent all day thinking, shadow boxing and doing push ups and of course I would read a little out of the Bible at night.

THE FIRST VISITING DAY

I was very nervous about seeing Deborah. I wanted to reassure her that I was fine and that I was controlling and handling the situation even if I had to fake it. The guards came and got me and lead me across the yard. It was a beautiful spring morning and I thought about the fact that I've never paid any attention to a beautiful spring morning before and how I wished that I was somewhere else besides this place, with Deborah enjoying this beautiful spring day.

Why wasn't I home waking up with my wife instead of being here waiting for her to come to see me? How will she look? Will I be able to contain myself or will my emotions take control?

They took me to the gym converted into the visiting gallery. There were a lot of seats but only a handful of inmates. It was a dreary place and the scent was like the scent of death. I waited in anticipation and fear. I knew I needed to smile as though everything was fine and I knew I had to be disciplined and well controlled. There was an iron gate that slid back and forth to let "free world" people in and out and I kept watching it waiting for her to come through. I felt a little sick; my heart was racing through my chest. God help me I want to see her and I don't want to see her.

AN ANGEL IN MY EYES

Then the door opened and there she stood. She looked as radiant as the morning sun and as lovely as the morning. She smiled and I smiled and we held each other and kissed. We talked positive about life. We talked about how we felt God was going to see us through and that we were going to make it. We didn't talk much about the case except that she was trying to talk to people to see if anything could be done about getting me out early. I saw her smile and I heard the positive tone in her voice but I could also see and feel the hurt. I missed her so much, how I desired to be away from here enjoying life as a free man but I wasn't and I couldn't. I had not been able to touch her in a month and I kept my hands on her the entire visit looking her in the eyes, which was something I hardly did before.

When the visit was over the inmates had to line up against the wall. I couldn't keep my eyes off of her; we waved and smiled at each other as we walked off. I started getting sick all over again. I didn't even want to see her walking back to her car.

"Man you got a good looking lady there, was that your wife?" the guard asked me; I didn't respond I just kept walking. I wanted to scream and run for the fence but seeing that razor wire changed my mind. My eyes started to fill up with tears but I forced them back down. My heart felt heavy and my stomach felt as though it had a hole in it. Oh how I wished that I could've held her just a little longer, all night would have been fine.

I had feelings of joy and pain; I was glad to see her and I felt like she was glad to see me but it was for so little time and under such abnormal circumstances. I went back to my cell and collapsed on the bed. I had no appetite or strength; I didn't know how I was going to handle being in prison but I knew that God had saved my life and I knew it was for a reason.

I thought about her all night; I wanted to be with her. It was so hard lying there separated from the woman that I loved so deeply. Oh God, how am I going to make it? How am I going to deal with prison?

THE THOUGHTS OF FREEDOM

I hadn't realized how precious freedom was. Freedom to love, to embrace, to talk to someone when you wanted to, just to go outside on the porch or to walk around the block in the cool of the day; to go to the refrigerator for a drink of water; to bathe or shower when you wanted to; To feel the wind of freedom on my face. To hold my wife in my arms and tell her how much I love her seemed to be the dearest thing in the world, but I couldn't and it hurt desperately. I no longer wanted to end my life but I longed to sleep until this was over.

Chapter 10

DEALING WITH DESPAIR

ANOTHER MOVE

Days and nights went by slowly; I couldn't keep my mind off of being outside the fence that kept me separated from the rest of the world. They eventually moved me to another unit – unit 15. They moved me in with an older man as mean as a snake. He had cut up a young man for spitting on him. He had been given 3 years and would only have to do less than a year.

I didn't know what to expect from him, but later found out that he was slightly ill. Living in the cell with him was hard; he smoked a pipe and always waited until our cell doors were locked. The smoke was asphyxiating; it was as though I was going to die of suffocation.

MY FIRST CONFRONTATION

I'd asked him once if he would wait until we went outside but the cold hard look that he gave me told me that he could care less about my feelings or me. He smoked his pipe almost all night one night, and I struggled with the desire to jump off the top bunk, push that pipe down his throat and let him choke to death. I was telling myself if this is what I have to do to survive in here then I have to survive, then another voice came "I will not put on you more than you can bare." I said, "Lord I can't take this, I can't breath, I can't sleep and I can't even reason with this man, help me please!"

The next morning at breakfast they came and moved him to another unit for inmates with the same mental condition. All I could do was say "thank you Jesus"; I knew it was a prayer answered. I felt the presence of God with me and it enabled me to realize that He was truly a prayer answering God. I was able to sleep in peace the next few nights until the loneliness started to creep back in.

THE PAIN OF LONELINESS

I didn't just have a need for a woman I wanted my wife. I wanted to talk to her, to see her, to hold her, and to make sure she was okay. I wanted to talk to my daughter and be there for her when she needed an answer to her problems. None of that was possible except over the phone and on visitation days and it was just not enough. I kept asking myself "what have I done to deserve this kind of punishment"? When I looked around and saw so many other guys that were real criminals and had committed far worse crimes than I, it was beyond understanding how their time was a fourth of mine, and anyone could tell that some of them had no purpose in life but to commit crimes.

I felt so out of place, I had completely changed from the person I used to be, my life was well, I was harming no one, I was a happy man with a family trying to make an honest go of life. Why now, five years after the fact, why was it so necessary to incarcerate me? I was tried and found guilty of armed robbery and the guilty must pay and that's all that mattered.

OVERKILL

I wanted so badly to get to someone, anyone who could help because this is just not fair. It appeared as though nothing mattered to the system, they didn't care anything about my family nor did they care about me.

I was being punished not for who I was but for something I had done a long time ago. I pled not guilty from the start because the timing was just completely off. I had told no one and I had forgotten about it for a year and a half until I was stopped for a traffic violation and the warrant was discovered.

I had already altered my lifestyle and my life, with new friends who knew nothing of my past. They thought I was someone special and different. I didn't have the nerve to disclose my criminal past to such an unsuspecting bunch.

No one knows why it took so long to arrest me but later I felt it must have been the will of the Lord; had I been arrested before I met my wife, prison would not have mattered because I would have never known life with her. I wouldn't have had such a strong desire for freedom and would have never prayed for help from God.

When I was arrested no one could believe that I had committed an armed robbery. This made it very difficult for me to admit. Everyone thought I was a happy go lucky guy that wouldn't hurt anyone. They never saw or witnessed my dark side that came to an abrupt end when I started doing stand up comedy 5 months after that particular robbery.

Chapter 11

FROM COPING TO HOPING

People grow through experience if they meet life honestly and courageously. This is how character is built.

Eleanor Roosevelt (1884 - 1962), My Day

COPING WITH GUILT

Although I knew I was guilty I never thought that I'd be found guilty and this would just be an ugly episode in the life of and upcoming comedian. What did I do? I wished I could go back now and plead guilty and throw myself on the mercy of the court and probably receive probation; but I couldn't go back and I didn't have probation, I was found guilty and received a 12 year prison term. "God help me", would I loose the only thing in this life that was worth living for? The separation was eating at me like a cancer. I hated going to bed at night, I hated waking up in the mornings, I hated sitting in the cell hour on hour, and it was driving me crazy. The walls were caving in.

GOD SENT HELP

It was nice and pretty outside and I wanted to be out there, this is really a life for an animal, it's not meant for a man. My head was ringing; I wanted out, I'm going to explode. God help me please! As my eyes filled with tears my cell door opened and an officer came in and told me that I would start outside on garbage detail in the morning. "Praise the Lord", a prayer answered again without delay. I couldn't wait to tell Deborah what happened to let her know that the Lord was indeed with us.

Just to be able to go outside sometimes would help me so much. I was so glad not to have to stay in that cell all day, every day. Having outside privileges gave me the opportunity to work on my case in the Law Library. The Supreme Court had also turned down my case so I was filing a Post Conviction Relief and there was an inmate Lawyer helping me. I was trying desperately to get out. Every let down felt like a vicious punch in the gut. It took all the strength out of me, I wanted to get out everyday and couldn't see my surviving years feeling as I did.

The Post Conviction Relief brought up several issues, but the one in particular that caused me much uneasiness with the

Justice System, is the method they use to retrieve a "positive" identification.

On the day of my Parliamentary Hearing, I was sitting in the courtroom with at least a hundred other people, with Deborah sitting beside me.

I saw my attorney from the Public Defender's office conversing with the District Attorney along with the Detective for the Public Defenders. My Attorney walked off and soon returned in front of me with the District Attorney, the Detective and the girl I had robbed. Standing in front of me with the victim, one of them pointed at me and asked her if I was the guy that robbed her. She looked at me emotionless and they all walked off.

My Attorney came back and told me that she said I was the one but my hair and glasses were different.

I tried to suppress the identification before trial but everyone involved testified that they stood the victim in front of the courtroom and she pointed me out while I was sitting in the back of the courtroom. I never was able to make the Judge believe otherwise.

THEN CAME HOPE

Life in prison was torment, I felt as though I was being punished beyond measure. It was still hard to believe that all I'd lived and done has resulted to this. I was hoping that the judge would hear my case again and give me a new trial or a time cut or something. A Post Conviction Relief was relief after your conviction stating issues you feel were wrong during the trial. An inmate Lawyer helped me to get back in court and I felt as though I was going to get out of this. After sending all my papers in it took about three months before I heard anything.

I was desperately anxious and praying, as I'd never prayed before. They appointed me an Attorney that came to see me but didn't seem too interested. He told me he couldn't understand how I was convicted on such a case and that everything looked winnable. I was elated and exhorted I knew that God was going to get me out this way.

ANOTHER DAY IN COURT

A court date was set to hear my Post Conviction Relief. My dad, a few friends, and Deborah were there. She looked so good when I saw her it seemed as though time slowed down. She moved like crystal clear water in a slow moving stream. I had to quickly look away to keep myself together.

The case was heard, I testified, Deborah and a couple of character witnesses who were not allowed to testify at the original trial testified also. My heart was beating fast I knew everyone in the courtroom could hear it. I was sitting in the same seat and the same courtroom and with the same judge where I was convicted a year and a half ago. I was about ready to scream; my attorney was not effective at all but the judge said, "I'll take this matter under advisement." I didn't quite know what that meant but it wasn't "denied; next case."

We left the courtroom; I didn't look back at my wife I just looked ahead. It really would've been nice if I could've left with them for home instead of having to return back to my nightmare. It was very difficult not knowing how long the judge was going to take my case under advisement and the anxiety was burning inside me.

A DESPERATE NEED FOR PRAYER

I was out on the yard sweeping and praying I wanted so much for someone to pray with and for me. One day I saw the Chaplain walking by, I needed prayer desperately or I felt like I would scream. I stopped him and asked him if he would pray with me. "I need prayer badly," I said. What he said to me shocked me, I know I had a look of desperation on my face but he told me to sign up to see him in my unit and it'll probably take about 2 days and he walked off. I was devastated and almost cried and I realized that I had to seek the Lord's help for myself. I never talked to that Chaplain again for anything.

I couldn't believe it. He was supposed to be a man of God willing to help; but it seemed as though he had no compassion at all. I felt horrible as I watched him walk off never even turning around to take a second look. My eyes filled up with water, my heart felt heavy, "I want to go home, please God help me" I would think about my family every minute, evenings and nights were the worst; depression and loneliness would set in.

Chapter 12

INSIDE OUTSIDE

GOD SEEMED TO BE WORKING

I had already been classified to go to the Turney Center, another prison about an hour away from Nashville but I didn't want to go. It would have been too difficult for Deborah to get there and I didn't want anything to be more difficult than it already was.

One day I was working on the yard sweeping and I noticed the head kitchen director watching me. He walked over to me and asked me if I would try out for a job in the kitchen. I accepted immediately, praise God maybe I will get an opportunity to stay here and move to another unit and have some regular hours outside my unit. I started working the next day actually it was a probationary job position to see if he would keep me on permanent. It was a hard job, washing dishes, all of the dishes, but I didn't mind. I felt as if it was a blessing from God.

UNPLEASANT THINGS HAPPENING OUTSIDE

A lot of things were happening on the outside. Mom and Dad were separated and going through a divorce. My baby sister had gotten married and her husband was physically abusing her, and I felt helpless; not to mention the things my wife and daughter were going through. It was really difficult to try to maintain myself from day to day.

THE REACTION TO A FIGHT

It seemed as though the other inmates there were right at home. Was I the only one feeling hurt and depressed? They didn't seem to have a problem in the world. Most of the time it was like television, they looked rough and murderous and they were. There were fights regularly. One guy got thrown through a glass door, picked up glass in both hands and started cutting at the other one. Before I knew it I jumped between them and grabbed both hands of the guy with the glass. Inmates all over the unit never let me forget how stupid that was, I could have been killed. I really knew I was changing because I normally would have wanted to see someone hurt or killed and would have possibly been involved in either or both myself. But I'm not the same guy that I used to be. I'm not the same young fool that didn't have a future or any morals or respect for the other person. I've gotten older and wiser. I have a family and a career. I have feelings now, why can't they realize I don't belong here? God help me make them see.

Inmates and guards both would constantly ask me "man what did you do to get locked up? You just don't seem like you belong here," and it would hurt even more, because I felt the same way.

THE KITCHEN

The job in the kitchen was strange. I had to get up extremely early in the morning, about 3:30 a.m. It was always pleasant then; I never knew it could seem so peaceful that early, it still hurt because I would rather have been leaving my own house, going to a job on the outside than leaving a cell going to another building in prison.

There was never a morning that I didn't pray and ask God to keep my family safe and to keep my wife strong and to protect me in this den of lions. The kitchen director had to agree to keep me in order for me not to get shipped out of town to another prison. He would weed out whom he wanted when their shipping day came and have them reclassified by the Warden. I'd seen them cry when they left for Fort Pillow or Turney Center. The director wouldn't vouch for them and they went, many crying like babies.

Chapter 13

SOFT ANSWERS AND SMALL PRAYERS

TIME STOOD STILL

I really didn't think it mattered where you were locked up; your freedom was still a distant past or a far off future. I wanted to stay in Nashville for Deborah's sake, so I prayed that the kitchen director would find favor in me and keep me.

It was early one Wednesday morning, I was up and out of my unit like before eagerly anticipating visitation that evening.

The kitchen director hadn't come to work at all the week prior nor had he come any this week, his daughter had suffered a car accident, and his heart was at home with her. I had prayed constantly for her after I found out.

I had not expected anything unusual that day, so everything that transpired was a total shock. I was doing my job as always when the phone rang, one of the assistant kitchen directors was there and yelled out "Walton report to your unit you're shipping out to Turney Center".

My heart stopped beating, I couldn't move, panic rushed through me, I really thought I was going to pass out. I can't go right now, how would I get word to Deborah, she'd worry not knowing what had happened to me. I tried not to show how scared I was, things had happened to other inmates this same way and some of them even cried. I wasn't about to cry but I didn't want to go.

The sergeant who got me the job was running around trying to get something done but it was useless, only the main kitchen director could speak up and say he wanted to keep me, and then he would have to fill out some paperwork, there was nothing anyone could do.

The unit guard was calling every five minutes "get Walton down here now!" I couldn't move, I just stood there watching all the other inmates watching me, some were even mocking me saying "where's your God now?"

The telephone started ringing again the kitchen assistant said "you'd better go" and about that time a guard came through the door looking very angry, the assistant pointed me out and he started toward me in an angry stomp, but before he was able to get to me the main director came through the door and said "he's okay I've taken care of him up front."

Everything seemed to start up again because for a while it seemed like time stopped, with all that was going on, I seem not to be able to say or do anything.

The Lord had once again shown His handiwork in my life in this place. Everyone I could get to, I let them know what God had done for me that day.

SIX-FIVE AND A CHIP ON HIS SHOULDERS

Every time the Lord blessed me, it seemed like it angered the devil. There was a guard who was about 6ft 5 all indications of a raciest, tried hard to find a reason to get on to me, but I always made sure I stayed out of trouble with the guards, especially, this one.

This guard was loud and rude; he always made a big scene with everything, when it was time for his shift he would make sure everyone knew he was there, by yelling and swearing at someone he thought feared him, mostly blacks.

I guess because I never appeared to be effected by his presence or his size, and the fact that I was new, he looked for an opportunity to use me as an example.

One day after I had moved my stuff into the unit where all the inmates stayed who worked on the compound, I was standing talking inside the door of the unit.

All of a sudden that guard came from nowhere and started yelling, I didn't know who he was yelling at until our eyes met." What the h— are you doing over here? You know d— well this is off limits to you, now you get you're a– back to your unit now!"

He was coming towards me yelling vehemently pointing his finger at my face. A feeling that my life was being threatened suddenly came over me and before I knew it I was in self-defense mode in my mind, ready to physically defend myself if needed.

I had always objected to the way he brought havoc to each unit when he showed up so it didn't take much for me to have a serious problem with him. Because he was a guard and I was a criminal he had the advantage, because I wanted to be free one day, I had to remember where I was and whom I was trying to please.

A scripture came to my mind, "a soft answer turns away wrath" so I spoke softly back to him, never taking my eyes off him, never backing up, never changing my facial expression. I said, "I moved in today sir". He stopped yelling, but at the risk of being defeated, he ordered me in the guard's office to check the logbook. When he opened the book I immediately saw my name and hit the place on the page where it was with my finger, he looked up at me, I looked at him, I'm sure he knew I was upset, but I turned and walked off. That guard never again approached me in a negative way.

A SURPRISING ANSWER TO A SMALL PRAYER

Life in prison was unpredictable; I never knew what was going to happen from one day to the next, and at times from one hour to the next.

I had several cellmates most charged with some type of drug use or possession; one was a Muslim who persuaded me to start studying Islam.

Islam was an interesting religion, but it didn't seem to give me that inward change I so desperately needed, but on the other hand neither did Christianity seemed to change those inmates that called themselves Christians, even the Chaplin told dirty jokes. I didn't hang around many of them and said nothing to the Chaplin at all. I went to hear him on a few Sunday mornings in the chapel but felt as if he didn't speak on issues that concerned our hurts and needs.

I read the bible and prayed that the Lord would help me to change, to be a better person than I was, and to be a light, even in here. I guess it was working, inmates started coming to me for prayer concerning everything from outside concerns to parole hearings.

Prayers seemed to have been answered every time I prayed, but my heart stayed heavy because I was tired of being incarcerated. The more prayers I saw answered the more anxious I became, the more my expectations grew and the harder it was for me to get up and go to work every morning.

"God you've got to do something, this just doesn't make any sense, why am I here? O' yea I remember, I'm a desperate criminal, who needs to be off the streets".

I played basketball to help with tension, one night while playing I sprained my ankle so badly I needed assistance getting back to the unit. I barely could get to the shower and back, and making it to my top bunk was even more difficult, but I managed. After getting settled I realized if I went to the clinic tomorrow they would put me on crutches, and tomorrow was visitation. If

Deborah saw me on crutches she would surely worry, and I didn't want that. My ankle was swollen almost double sized and it hurt something awful. I said a simple prayer, "Lord I don't want my ankle swollen tomorrow please heal it in Jesus name thank you amen" and I went to sleep.

The next morning I leaped off the top bunk as usual and about half way down I remembered my ankle, but when my feet hit the floor, all the swelling and pain had gone. I couldn't believe it, just like that God heard and answered without hesitation. I couldn't wait to tell someone, but as usual some believed and some didn't believe my ankle was ever hurt that badly. God answering that prayer gave me more confidence that God was hearing me and that I would soon be released from this dungeon.

TRUE DEDICATION

Visitation and telephone privileges were really the only thing inmates could find any real pleasure in or look forward to. Deborah would come every Wednesday and every weekend, on Saturdays she would get there at eight o'clock in the morning and stay until about four that evening, with an hour break between twelve and one. I was amazed at her dedication especially after working eight hours a day for five days prior. I felt so bad for her, but I needed her there so desperately. Those visits meant so much to me, but it hastened my desire for freedom even more.

It would take me days to get over the emotional impact of the visit, because every time she left, a part of my heart left with her, and I longed to leave with her.

There were times when I wished she would go and start her life over, but I didn't know how I would function if she left me now. God help me, how will I make it if I had to do this time, and how will Deborah hold up if she realized that I was going to spend years in here.

Most of the time after weekend visits, drugs would be plentiful and most of the inmates would almost act as if they were on the streets partying. I would go sat up on my bunk and with tears coming down, wonder what was going to happen to my life and what is my little family doing now at this moment. I felt so far from home I just couldn't stand it.

I got regular visits from other family members including my father and his new wife, which was very difficult because my mother hurt so badly from their divorce.

When you meet your antagonist, do everything in a mild and agreeable manner. Let your courage be as keen, but at the same time as polished, as your sword.

Richard Brinsley Sheridan (1751- 1816)

Chapter 14

SEASONS CHANGE

HOLIDAY HEARTACHES

Everyday I anticipated something from the courts, with the Lord answering my prayers on the regular basis; I just knew I was getting out soon. With the issues I presented to the judge and the time factor I felt confident that the Lord would use this to get me out early. I didn't understand why it was taking so long for the judge to respond, it'd been months now, Christmas was around the corner and I didn't want to be here for Christmas.

A more sickening feeling came over me as the holidays approached, this was definitely not a merry time for me. My wife's birthday was in November also Thanksgiving and then Christmas, not to mention our wedding anniversary in January. What a horrible thing to have happen to a man when those days mean so much.

I knew at a certain time the courts would close down, and reopen after the new year, so I desperately hoped and prayed that something would happen before then...but nothing happened.

The months passed right on by and I felt like the bottom part of my body was weighted down by a tremendous burden. My energy left me and a haze came over the whole prison. I felt like I was the invisible man who nobody saw and nobody cared about.

We had to get up at four am to go to the kitchen to start cooking for the entire compound. Seeing the stars out on a cold winter morning would drain more life out of me. I was always thinking about my wife at home asleep and how I longed to be there with her, but instead I was miles away doing time. What a dreadful experience for a man in love.

THE MESSENGER OF SATAN

There was always something happening to keep me off balance. There was an inmate there sent from hell, I called him the messenger of Satan to hassle me. He was a medium build black guy who had been transferred from a place called The Farm back to our close security institution. He had been locked up for eight calendar years and only had about a year left. Most of the other inmates knew him from "The Walls" so he played up the fact that this place was a boys camp, and most of us wouldn't make it at a real prison," especially that nigga' over there. It seems as though he was trying to lure me into some type of confrontation with him, but I didn't say anything, I just looked at him every now and then with plain cold stares. He didn't know me, but he watched me get mail and my nightly phone use and knew I went to visit often and used it to torment me.

It appeared as though his ultimate desire was to depress me into suicide or at the least a nervous breakdown. He would come up to me or walk past me or stand behind me in certain lines and pour out a flood of negativity, such as; "you're playing the oldest con game in the penitentiary trying to ride the Bible out, and all them letters you getting they gone stop, your visits they gone stop too, she probably done already got a man, you crazy if you thank she gone wait for you, ask anybody in here women don't stay with a man more than a few months and if they do they'll get outta bed with someone and come right out here and see you."

I walked away when I could and other times I'd pretend that he was not affecting me at all.

I was deeply affected by most of the things he said, I was wrestling with my own thoughts I didn't need anyone else feeding them. The things he said caused me to have terrible dreams that made it very difficult for me to properly function the next day. I always made sure that when this guy was around I didn't give him any indications that he was really getting to me.

During the day I kept an emotionless look, neither smiling nor looking sad, but at night my tears became my pillow when my heart was overwhelmed. I tried hard to think pleasant thoughts but at night when there was no one around my mind would run a course of self pity and loneliness to the point that I'd hurt inside.

The messenger of Satan started getting agitated that I seemed not to be bothered by him and his negative remarks concerning my life. He seemed to have begun to get more verbal than ever and even his anger became stirred. One day he walked up to me and said, "if we were at The Walls you'd be my girlfriend" that statement went all over me. I was washing dishes at the time and I wanted to hit him with something, anything. I didn't look up I kept washing dishes, but I wanted him to know what I thought about that statement. I said "why don't you just pretend like you're at The Walls, and I just turned and looked at him and as soon as our eyes met, inmates around us grabbed me and moved me away from him and started encouraging me about how he wasn't worth me losing out on my freedom for. I appreciated what they had done, but I really didn't think he was as tough as he wanted me to believe. As upset as I was at the time I really didn't care. Only God knows how close I came to getting another case that would have kept me locked up probably for life. I didn't know how much more of this I could take, before I did something I would regret for the rest of my life. It seemed as though someone was always present to say something to him when he started harassing me. Thank God he never put his hands on me.

THE THOUGHTS OF ESCAPING

It was closing in on March 1985, one year of incarceration. How I stumbled through one year is beyond my comprehension, how I made it through the holidays is an even bigger mystery. I remembered a few months back when the doors of the unit opened for us to go outside for recreation. A young man burst out from behind me and ran like a madman directly toward the fence, it was so sudden that the guard took a while to scream for him to stop. He scaled up the side of the fence and jumped over the first fence, but didn't have enough momentum to make it over the second one and was caught in the razor sharp wire and was hanging there still trying hard to make it over. We were rushed back inside and didn't know how they got him down nor ever heard anything else about him.

I could see how things could get that difficult for a person to the point that they would take any chance they could to escape. The thought would often come to my mind, but I always wondered, then what, where would I go, what would I do, what kind of life would I have?

I just missed my family, if I escaped I still couldn't spend any time with them, besides if I didn't make it, I'd get more time away from them. It's a no win situation. I couldn't do anything but wait, hope and continue to pray that God would see my hurt and let me go home.

Although it had been a year I had not gotten use to being there, I still awoke every morning hurting deep down inside from the loneliness and the despair of wasting away in a merciless beast called justice.

DEBORAH'S CHANGE OF HEART

One thing that eased some of the pain was that Deborah was really getting serious about her relationship with God and had stopped going to the nightclubs. That alone gave me a little more security about our marriage. I was very familiar with the nightclub life and the atmosphere that it produced and the effect it could have on single or lonely people.

My oldest sister's pastor from Old Hickory, Tennessee, had begun to visit me and seemed to always come at the time when I couldn't go any further without some type of encouragement. We had deep discussions about baptism and the Holy Ghost. Although I had been raised to believe that the Bible teaches that speaking in other tongues was the evidence that one had the Holy Ghost, I had been introduced to so many other teachings, including Islam, I had become confused.

The Pastor was so wise in his approach, showing me what the Bible was really saying about being saved. Showing me through the Bible made me realize truth, regardless of what I thought. Eventually my sister started going back to her previous church in Nashville and had convinced Deborah to start going, which would ultimately alter the course of our lives forever.

SPRINGTIME

Springtime, here again I was being reminded of the first few days I was there and how I felt then, which is really not too much different from now. I should be enjoying walking in the park, evening cookouts talking with my wife in the cool of the day. I should be waking up in my own house with my family, kissing my wife and daughter as we departed from each other to begin our day. I really miss that.

I wondered how they were doing and how they felt when they really needed me and I wasn't there. I wondered if they missed me as much as I missed them. I wondered if Deborah was thinking about moving on with her life, I wondered until it hurt to wonder, so I tried to think other thoughts of how I would survive and maintain if they ceased to remain there for me. Springtime is a time when love is strong in the atmosphere, but it's a miserable sickening feeling when you're locked up. It may be a boy's camp for some, and I realize also that I could be in a far worse place but I couldn't see how any prison could make me feel any worse than I felt then.

I constantly wondered how Deborah was really doing, and how she was really feeling about our separation and future.

Chapter 15

IT'S GOOD FOR THE SOUL

THE MASKS WE WORE

In a years time I could really see through some of the other inmate's masks. They would try to calm themselves by pretending that they were not concerned about their wives or girlfriends, by making jokes about what they were doing and whom they were doing it with. I didn't find any of those conversations humorous and tried to stay away from the areas where they were being discussed. I had enough to deal with from the messenger of Satan, and my own dreams and nightmares.

Some of the guys would try to lure me into a discussion about my marriage on a one- on- one bases but I would alter the conversation by talking about trusting God, never allowing my emotions to show my own real concerns. I tried to talk strong faith talk and encourage others to keep the faith in spite of my own doubts and insecurities.

Nighttime lock-downs were extremely hard; I would lie on my bunk and hear the guard locking the doors. With each turn of the lock it seemed like every bone in my body would quake as I stared at the ceiling until my eyes got heavy.

I didn't want any pictures of my family; this was something I didn't want to deal with. Missing them terribly and seeing their pictures everyday seemed like it would be torture. Seeing them every time I closed my eyes and all during the day, remembering the times we did share together and feeling sad about the times wasted doing other things.

Sometimes I could hardly breath just thinking, wondering what this time would be like if I had never fallen in love. Love, why now when my freedom seems an eternity away?

HOPE DEFERRED

The feeling of loneliness is a real pain that grabs you in the pit of your stomach until it decides to let go. On most occasions, emotions would push the tears out sometimes uncontrollably. Thank

God it was mostly at night when all the lights were out and no one could see my weakness.

I felt that both Deborah and I, were anticipating something happening in court that could have me home before long so maybe she would stick with me and not fold up. I kept thinking that as long as she thought that something was around the corner she would stick around, but if she actually knew I would be here for a while she wouldn't be able to commit to staying with me.

Hope surely kept us looking everyday for a positive reply from court, every time I saw some one come from operations I thought they might be coming for me. Unfortunately that hope was killed, when I received a letter from the judge's office. The sun was about to go down when the mail came and when I looked at the envelope a big lump came in my throat, I didn't know what to expect fear again engulfed me like a cold wet blanket. I walked slowly to my cell praying, "Please God please, don't let it be bad news I won't be able to handle it if it's bad news". My heart was pounding and sweat started pouring out, it seemed like it was taking me forever to open it. After opening the envelope I still didn't unfold the letter right away. I bowed my head and prayed. "Jesus please, make it right, please"!

I slowly opened the letter, it didn't take but a few sentences to realize it was not in my favor, as I read what seemed like my obituary, tears started falling on my glasses which caused me to get up and wash my face and compose myself. He turned down every issue I brought up and seemed to do it with ease, not caring that our very lives depended on this. What a devastating blow, if I had not been sitting down it would have knocked me to my knees. What a sock in the gut, I couldn't believe it, nothing good at all, not one thing. I felt like he deceived me, I left the courtroom that day believing he was going to give me some relief. I got mad at God, I'd been good I'd not committed any sins, or crimes, I've witness to others about Him, I had faith I was depending on Him to deliver me, what happened?

There's nowhere else I can appeal, this was my last option, and how on earth am I going to tell Deborah? I know she was expecting this to be over soon, this will surely cause her to close the book on us. I sat on the bunk with my head in my hands; it felt like my head was being pressed from both sides. I wanted to crawl in a hole somewhere and die, but there were no holes and I was once again left with the difficult job of informing my wife of hurting news that could alter her life.

A MESSAGE FROM GOD

The thing that had always helped me when I got into a crisis was to read something from Psalms. As I reached for my Bible, it slipped a little and fell in my lap, opened, immediately my eyes fell instantly on Isaiah 59 verses, 1, 2 & 3; "Behold, the Lord's hand is not shortened, that he cannot save; neither his ear heavy, that it cannot hear: But your iniquities have separated between you and your God, and your sins have hid his face from you, that he will not hear. For your hands are defiled with blood, and your fingers with iniquity; your lips have spoken lies, your tongue hath muttered perverseness." I knew it was a message from God, I had not claimed responsibility for my past crimes including the one I've now been convicted of. I had hoped it would somehow go away, but look at what has happened, I pleaded not guilty for a crime I was guilty of and was trying to even lie to God. I had blocked God's hand from helping and His ears from attending to my cries, I was lying to Godly people who were praying for me, I was expecting God to override His own justice to save me. I was so void of understanding to believe that I could con God.

I had to do something I had never done, admit to the horror of my past life. I was so ashamed of myself that I couldn't bring myself to say that I was that kind of person; cold, callus and hard-hearted, I would do anything to get what I wanted, or needed.

I know now, directly from God, that I had to deal with this issue by being truthful, if I ever expect anything from Him. I needed not only tell Deborah about the letter but the whole story, of my past life that she never knew.

BREAKING FREE

I had spent all this time blaming the Court System for their mishandling of my case, and telling myself that had they done things right, and if that "white woman" and her dad had not lied about the identification and the issues with the Public Defender and lawyers and the Prosecutors and Judge, I wouldn't be in this predicament.

I had to come to grips with myself and look at the "man in the mirror" to recognize that normal people don't do what I've done, and that concept made me realize that I had a serious problem. God immediately showed me after I excepted responsibility, the reason I had committed all those unspeakable things.

I had built up a hatred for my dad and the way I had been brought up and the bulling I had encountered through school, and it turned me into this monster to make up for it.

Wow! I thought it was just the past, I never thought that I would've ever been affected by those incidences in that manner. However when God revealed it to me, I could see plainly what it had done and why.

God healed me completely that night even though I felt that I could never forgive, He helped me because I asked Him to. All of that went through my mind and it felt as though I was being set free from years of emotional bondage.

Now to continue the freedom process, I had to expose myself to those who had put so much confidence in me.

THE TIME TO CONFESS

I felt in my heart that the truth would surely end my marriage; I have deceived my wife, both of our families, my lawyers and even myself. I even got my wife's grandmother to put her house up for my bond after my conviction. So many people believed in me, so many could never imagine me doing something so wrong. I knew I was guilty but couldn't bring myself to admit it.

I've betrayed the people who thought so much of me, and caused them to put their lives on the line for a lie. Deborah had put so much faith in my innocence that she almost stopped her own life and had gone in so much debt trying to help me get out. Although I knew I probably deserved prison, I still had no right to bring that kind of burden on her.

Although I felt like my life, as I knew it on the outside was over, I was beginning to feel unusually free on the inside. It was strange, I was about to lose everything I held dear to me, and I was experiencing an inside freedom I've not known since I'd been there.

I knew what I had to do, and I tried to think spiritually, in that my relationship with God was more important than anything, but in reality I knew very little about a relationship with God, and everything about my relationship with my wife.

I began to get very nervous and I guess it was showing. Another inmate, who had spent many years in prison before, and was back in for a little while, really helped me with my prayer life and overall spirituality. I believe God sent him to me, he helped me to talk about what I had done and other crimes I had committed, it was almost like confession. When I had finished he told me that the devil was a lie, my wife was not going to leave me because of this. I had not told him my fears; I knew it had to be God.

I decided to wait for Wednesday's visitation to tell Deborah everything. No matter what I felt I knew from God, I was still sick from the fear of what might happen. I kept imagining her just getting up from visiting and walking out, never to see her again. The thought of that caused my stomach to hurt and I was having a hard time keeping from screaming. The thought of living without her was almost an unbearable thought, but the thought of her marrying someone else was even worse.

THE HARDEST THING I HAD EVER DONE

It was a fight for me up until visitation began; I finally realized that if I ever wanted God to be a positive force in my life, I had to come clean about everything, no matter what.

I decided to be completely emotionless, as I spilled my insides to the woman that meant more to me than life itself. I wanted her to make her mind up based totally on her own feelings, and not feeling sorry for me. I felt I was prepared for her to do anything, and I wouldn't blame her one bit.

She sat there for a minute and looked at me not smiling or looking sad, and then she told me that she had started suspecting that I must have been guilty since no prayers were being answered concerning my release. The letter from the judge really hurt her but she was at least relieved to know the truth, and at last direct the prayers in the proper direction.

It was nothing like I had anticipated, she was hurt but said nothing about leaving me to start her life over. What she now wanted to pray about was a miracle of an early release or to be transferred to a lower security facility. I was in awe at her determination, and wandered if I deserved such a remarkable woman. It made me realize how Blessed I was to have someone that was willing to stand by me in this manner, even after knowing the truth about my distorted past.

I walked around for days after that still not believing what had happened, and expecting that when she had time to think about it, she would no longer take my calls and end the visits and send a letter of divorcement. Although she had some questions and some ill feelings about some things, she was willing to tough it out with me, and I loved her even more for that.

We knew we could no longer seek justice for an innocent man, but mercy for one that was guilty. I told my oldest sister when she came to visit and wrote my mom and dad, everyone was glad I had at least confessed. No one seemed to react the way I thought they would. My sister even hugged me and told me she loved me. If I had known things would have been like this I probably would have confessed at the beginning. I guess all of this is in some sort of master plan of God's.

Chapter 16

NEW LIFE

COMMITTING TO A NEW WAY OF LIFE

Summertime 1985 was now on the horizon, the Lord was really blessing Deborah, she had recently gotten baptized in the Name of Jesus and the same night had received the baptism of the Holy Ghost with the evidence of speaking in another tongue. This was an experience she had never known about until she started attending my sister's church in Nashville.

This seemed to be the beginning of a new episode in our life, Deborah was really getting serious about God and that gave me a lot of relief. According to the Bible certain strengths came when a person receives the baptism of the Holy Ghost, and I felt like she really needed strength to deal with the hand she had been dealt at this time because of me.

Through all the doubts I previously encountered about Christianity I had come to realize it was what I needed because according to the Bible it was the only way. In order for me to believe that Jesus was the only way, I had to believe in the book that taught about Him. In the book that spoke of Him I was told that any other way would lead me on a path of destruction.

Ultimately I made arrangements with the prison and with the Pastor of the church in Old Hickory to be baptized. In May of 1985, I was taken to the "Walls" and was baptized in the Name of Jesus and about three weeks later I received the baptism of the Holy Ghost. As it turned out at the time I was between cellmates and did not have one at that particular time. What that did was give me a chance to pray out loud without offending anyone.

FILLED WITH THE HOLY GHOST

I had been praying since my baptism in water, and was beginning to get a little discouraged, because I had not yet been filled with the Holy Ghost, but I was determined. Before I started my praise session, I read the Bible verses pertaining to individuals speaking in tongues when they received the Holy Ghost. This night when

I reached to get my Bible it slipped out of my hands just like before, and fell opened at the same place as before, but this time my eyes immediately fasten on chapter 60 verses 1 & 2; "Arise, shine; for thy light has come, and the glory of the Lord is risen upon thee. For, behold, the darkness shall cover the earth, and gross darkness the people: but the Lord shall arise upon thee, and his glory shall be seen upon thee." Just like before I knew it was God, a joy overwhelmed me and when I opened my mouth to say thank you Lord, my praise went to another level, and before I knew what was happening I could hear myself speaking in another language. The more I spoke the more joyful I got. I believe I spoke continuously for almost an hour. I was like a man that had a little too much to drink when I staggered out of my cell to get some water.

I'm sure I looked peculiar, because someone asked me what was wrong with me. When I raised up to tell him it wouldn't come out plain, he said "you got the Holy Ghost" I put my hand over my mouth and ran back to my cell speaking in tongues all over again. I couldn't believe someone in here would know about the Holy Ghost.

My life and thoughts about life changed from that moment on. I was on an unexplainable high that I didn't want to come down from. For a time my physical freedom didn't seem to matter to me that much. If Deborah had this, she'll be all right for a while. I had so much joy I was telling my experience to everyone, even the messenger from Satan, who could no longer bother me with his negative conversations. I always had a Bible verse to quote him, that made him leave me alone. Most of the other inmates either didn't care or had never heard that there was a Holy Ghost.

The feelings I was having lasted for weeks. Deborah's and my conversations changed, we started praying more together and fasting together. This was great. We were starting on a journey together towards our eternity.

116

"GOD PLEASE"

The summer visits were held outside, it was a welcome change but the heat really bothered Deborah, but she kept insisting on coming. I often thought about all the trouble and discomfort I was causing in her life, and how much more would she have to endure if she decided to stay in this?

I felt really blessed to have such a beautiful woman standing by me, knowing what I had done to us. She got the full attention of all the other inmates when she came to visit, especially on Sundays. She looked like a princess who had just stepped out of a fairytale. I would always have a hard time sleeping at night after visits. I tossed and turned all night wanting to be home with her but knowing I couldn't and didn't know when I would be able to.

Although I appeared confident about our relationship, something deep inside me kept wondering how long before it ended. How long would she really wait? Inmates were getting letters from wives and girlfriends on the regular basis, and some would just stop showing up. I could always tell when it was bad news or when the absence would hurt to the core. They would try hard to pretend not to be bothered but I could see the sadness behind the smile.

I would sometimes overhear inmates yelling and cussing at their women, asking whom she had in bed with her. They even went as far as threatening her if they ever found out. Some would even slap the ladies in the visiting gallery. I never understood why he even expected her to come and see him after treatment of that sort.

I didn't consider myself the smartest man in the world, but I wondered sometimes how it would be if the tables were turned, and the women were locked up and we were out. How difficult would it be for me to stay faithful to Deborah whom I loved and was unable to be with and didn't know when I would?

I tried at times to convey that concept to some of the other inmates in order to make them aware of how difficult it must be for their women. Most of the time putting us in their position caused us even more discomfort than ever. Most of us realized that the temptations would be greater than we could comprehend, especially being a man. Although I knew that the Holy Ghost was power, was it enough to dilute human emotions and needs?

Whatever was going on in our heads we were all blessed to have any woman willing to walk with us a part of the way. Coming to grips with these realities sealed the fact that it's more than just our freedom, it's really our whole lives that have been altered, and only by the grace of God will we be able to resume any type of life after prison.

We all were battling inner wars that we couldn't share with anyone in its totality, so we had to fight them ourselves, and some were casualties of their own wars. Some were not able to handle the pressure and eliminated themselves one way or the other, just to end the pain.

The thoughts I had about prison never included the agony of the mental and emotional strain families endure because of a loved one incarcerated.

Most of the criminal type mentality had left me years ago, and even the crime itself was so long ago, it was still so hard to feel as though I deserved all this. Punishment I could accept, but this was overkill. I felt like the punishment was more than I could bare. I would still almost become sick but I'd suck it up, take a deep breath and try to make it through another day. "God please" is sometimes all I had strength to say.

Working in the kitchen was becoming a real challenge; they were stealing food all around me, and not only food, but also stuff to make penitentiary wine. I don't know why, but I was feeling very uncomfortable with all that trouble that close to me, knowing that if they got caught I'd also be blamed with them, and I didn't want any friction that could hinder me from getting out.

They were running a complete delicatessen out of the kitchen to who ever wanted to buy meals after regular dinner hours. They were making a lot of money and trades, and the more they made the more they stole, and the more uncomfortable I was getting, especially when they were getting things out of the pans I was working in.

I couldn't understand why they would continue to be led by the same spirit that cost them their freedom in the first place. Everyday something was happening that caused me to be more involved in their activities, not to mention the air of violent tension looming on the horizon.

A VERY PRESENT HELP

I desperately needed something to happen, I kept praying for some door to open so that I could be relieved from the horror house. Even some of the guys I thought were trying to do better would themselves get involved in doing things that could have jeopardized their freedom. I felt like a man on an island, alone and isolated in a world where I didn't fit.

A job opening became available in the prison warehouse; the messenger of Satan made parole and left a vacancy. Only three inmates were allowed to work there, one in the office two in the warehouse. I didn't apply for it but everyone in the kitchen did, plus numerous others around the prison. I was hoping that maybe one of the main thieves would get it and break up the action in the kitchen.

I really didn't care about where I worked I just wanted to get out of prison altogether. I had only been working in the kitchen for a few months and had already gotten the top position, meat cooker; this was why everything got so difficult for me. I felt honored that the kitchen director, who was now a woman felt confident enough in me to do something I had never done. I guess in a way I had a since of loyalty to the position, and didn't want to hurt her feelings.

I was resting on my day off, praying and meditating when a female guard came and told me that the warehouse supervisor wanted to see me, I was shocked and wondered what was going on. I had no idea what was happening I had never said anything to anyone; as a matter of fact I didn't talk to any of the free world people at all. I guess they seemed to act as though they were so much better than we were, and I guess in a way they were, so I stayed clear of them.

As she was escorting me to the warehouse I could feel the cold hard stares of some of the other inmates wondering why I was being called up there not realizing that I was wondering also. I was a little nervous because his office was close to the front gate and I started shaking a little to be that close to the way out but can't go. When I went in his office I felt a wave of hostility so my mental and emotional defenses were up. He didn't speak so I didn't speak. He asked me why I was in prison, I told him as emotionless as I could. He seemed to almost spit at me as he was telling me how he had no sympathy for convicts, because someone robbed and beat his grandmother years ago.

He proceeded to tell me that the only reason I was sitting in front of him was because so many guards as well as inmates alike recommended me above others they were familiar with. I was amazed at his statements but tried not to show any emotions, I didn't want him to think he was doing me any favors, and besides I really didn't care about it. When he finished talking down to me he asked if it was something I would be interested in, I nodded my head and he told me when to start and I walked out.

When the kitchen supervisor found out that I was no longer in the kitchen she started yelling and cussing, swearing that this would be the last time the warehouse would steal one of her best people. I felt honored that she was making such a fuss over me but the honor was soon snuffed, because some of the other inmates thought I had inside pull to obtain a job that everybody wanted when I didn't even apply.

Some were even calling me a snitch because I was chosen, and I didn't have anything to do with it at all. This was not a comfortable position to be in especially when you're new on the job.

I take it as a man's duty to restrain himself.

Lois McMaster Bujold, Ethan of Athos, 1986

Chapter 17

TEMPTATIONS

A NEW JOB

The other inmate that worked in the warehouse was white and stocky, a little shorter than I was, he had been in and out of prison for a while, and really had a chip on his shoulder. The work it self was hard but it was a lot less stressful and hard work was no stranger to me. Russell was a hard worker, and always seemed to try to out work me; I guess he didn't realize we were supposed to have been working together. He would arrive at the warehouse very early, I guess to impress the supervisor.

I knew he didn't particularly like me, but I just did my job and tried to stay away from him as much as possible. He would always make remarks about the people up front being so familiar with me, I didn't say anything about it I just did my job.

He was somewhat of a bully; he only picked on those he felt like he could bluff, but feared some of the others that would probably hurt him. I had a serious problem with him after seeing some of the things he did and said to some of the nonviolent inmates. I was bullied when I was in high school, so I never could tolerate a bully.

After studying martial arts and doing a little boxing, I often had dreams about going back home looking up some of my old bullies just to repay them for what they had done to me. But I just never got around to it.

Trying to live through the Spirit has me in a trap, I could not give place to wrath, so I tried harder to stay under control at all times. Russell was a real test he was always saying things to me that he wouldn't say if I were one of the guys he feared. I overlooked a lot of his sarcasms, but wanted to give him a quick lesson on respect. Many times he didn't know how close he was to me losing everything and exploding it out on him.

He was stealing things every time he went down to make coffee for the warehouse and thought his threats was keeping me from exposing him, but I figured he'd get caught soon enough and if he didn't it wasn't harming me at all.

TO STEAL, OR TO FIGHT

One particular day while I was leaving work, I was approached by an inmate, who was very adamant about getting him something out of the warehouse. I rehearsed to him the same as I had said to others, "I'm determining not to repeat the same habits that caused me to be here". He seemed to be shocked that I told him no, he started walking toward me and pointed his finger in my face and demanded that I have it for him tomorrow. This is really starting to bother me, what is going on here why does every one seem to want to threaten me lately?

Lord where were these people when I wasn't trying to live right? He knew nothing about me and was trying to use a scare tactic on me, and I wasn't scared just angry. I looked at him, shook my head and walked off.

I was so upset I could hardly think straight, I felt like an angry animal waiting to be let out of his cage. Why was I going through all of this? Why did I have to put up with so much harassment? All I had to do was to show them that I was not weak and very well capable of taking any one of them if need be.

I prayed a different prayer that night, I told the Lord that I knew I wasn't suppose to fight but I can't continue to let people think they can just push me around and I'm not going to let anyone hurt me. It was an angry prayer because I felt like the Lord had forsaken me.

Stealing was out of the question, but I figured if he came to fight me, maybe I could use the defense of martial arts and not the offence. He was chubby and smoked; surely he would give out and stop without me having thrown a punch. I told the Lord that I was leaving the results up to Him, however He did it, but I wasn't going to allow anyone to hurt me.

Something inside me wanted to fight this guy just because of how he approached me at the beginning. I got up early the next morning prayed and went for breakfast. He gave me the look of death at breakfast, I didn't change my expression I just figured it was on; I ate and went on to work.

I knew the way I was feeling was inappropriate for how I was trying to live but I just couldn't shake it off. I just kept calling on the name of Jesus the whole morning. The work was strenuous that morning; I felt like I had worked out in a gym, I was pumped.

I still don't know why this particular guy upset me so, and why I was so ready to put my freedom and my relationship with God on the line, but I had a build up of rage inside me and I guess I was taking it out on him.

I walked down from the warehouse for lunch, and he was standing outside close to the entrance, "You got my stuff?" I stopped, looked at the ground in front of him, slowly scanned up his body with my eyes and stopped at his midsection. I tried to show no emotions but I could feel my face making a slight snarl. I never raised my head nor did I look him in the eye. "That issue was closed yesterday" I said, I turned my eyes forward and walked on inside the unit for lunch. He never said a word and never seemed upset about it. I was shocked; at first I thought it was because two of my friends were standing outside at the time, one was about six-six, the other was my size but stocky. Then I realized they didn't know anything about it so I realized it must have been the Lord. He just fixed everything.

The Lord was once again my very present help in time of trouble, and I thanked Him for it. The Holy Ghost was really proving to me that the power the Bible spoke of was real. The power to want to do the right thing, and to be able to restrain oneself in the mist of a flood of adversities. I realized the strain of being incarcerated brought out emotions I had controlled for years. Anger was consuming me now and there is nothing I can do to release it. If the Lord doesn't help me, it could very well cost me everything.

TROUBLE IN THE WAREHOUSE

Several months had passed and the Lord was really helping me deal with Russell, his attitude was sometimes unbearable not to mention his sarcasm and profanity. I know I'm in a prison but this guy was deliberately trying to push buttons.

One night I was unable to talk to Deborah before the phones cut off, Jaimee kept saying she wasn't there I got really frustrated and started having bad thoughts even to the point of having a nightmare that night and couldn't get back to sleep when it woke me up. I skipped breakfast and didn't even pray before I left the cell.

I was really up tight by the time I got to work and was not able to handle Russell as before. He was unusually foul and seemed more aggressive than ever. He was on the forklift and driving recklessly, he almost hit me, and I raised my voice and said with my finger pointing at him, "You need to watch it." Saying something to him seemed to send him over the edge. He jumped off the forklift right in front of me and started cussing and calling me names, threatening me and telling me how tired he was of me snitching to the people up front and how he ought to just kick my ass right here.

I started shaking all over with anger, I had to look slightly down at him, but I kept my head straight ahead. All I could hear in my mind was, "take him out" we were all alone, no one would blame me, everyone knew how he was. It wouldn't take much to hurt him but I knew that if I hit him I would have to kill him because of all the bulling he had done over the last few months. I really wanted to teach him a real lesson, and the longer I stood in front of him the angrier I became and the harder it was getting to just stand there without hitting. With every ounce of strength I had in me I turned and walked away from him toward my unit crying, because I couldn't understand why God would allow me to endure such pain and abuse at the hands of someone like this.

By the time I got to my cell I was crying like I had been beaten and collapsed on the bottom bunk and just started crying out to the Lord "please help me, please help me, I can't take any more of this." The scripture came to me to pray for them which despitefully use you and persecute you. It was one of the hardest things I had done, but I started praying for the Lord to touch his mind that he may come to know Him before it was too late. As I prayed I started feeling better and started recognizing the Lord's hand in that incident; Russell didn't get racial nor did he touch me in all his fury, surely that must have been the hand of the Lord. I realized what the devil was trying to do, but it didn't work.

A NEW FRIEND

I didn't go back to work until after lunch but when I went up there I had intentions on apologizing to him for our little misunderstanding, but before I could get up there, he came out and met me, apologizing to me. He had a couple of cold drinks and he began to tell me how sorry he was that he had caused me so much hell. "I ain't never met nobody like you man you must be for real with what you are trying to do." He told me he hoped that we could be friends; we shook hands and were good friends until he left for "The Farm".

The Lord always seemed to be at work even when I didn't feel him, or think he was there, He seemed to help me get out of every situation I found myself in. It was so amazing to me, one minute I'm ready to kill and a few minutes later we're shaking hands as friends. The Holy Ghost was a real power source that can guide, put peace and comfort inside a person whenever he needed it. It was so powerful I wasn't even upset about not being able to get in touch with Deborah. The Lord is really showing me Himself.

SELF-DEFENSE AND TEMPTATION

One of the most difficult things for me was trying to keep myself from using my martial arts when I seemed threatened, because most of the time I felt that the other person was really no match for me. Maybe I had too much confidence in myself but every since I started studying and competing, I had a sense of invulnerability when it came down to defending myself.

There was a day when tensions were extremely high, summer and fall over, winter and the holiday season on the horizon. There were very intense basketball games in the gym that night and the team I played on won most of the games. Some of the guys played like they were playing for parole and got very upset when they lost. I never argued I only played for the fun, so when fights would break out I just went to the sideline until it was over. A lot of fights broke out that night, but nobody got seriously injured. When the games were over I stayed behind to talk to one of my friends about his temper and how he really should think before he jumps.

I tried to dry off a little but the guard ran us out, and I ran back to my unit so I wouldn't be out in the cold too long. As I stepped in the unit I noticed a lot of the guys were standing outside their cells and it seemed a little quieter than usual. I didn't pay it any attention and proceeded to go to my cell, which was at the back of the unit. As soon as I was halfway through them someone said "get him" someone grabbed me around the neck from behind, my instinct caused me to push him backward against his cell door, and I moved my body a little and tapped him lightly in his groin, he immediately let me go and grabbed himself. I backed up against another cell door and waited to see what was going to happen. They all started laughing, I didn't know what was going on, and I got a little scared, cause the guy that grabbed me use to be a football player for some college, and was quite large. Some of my friends heard the commotion and came out ready to fight I assured them that we were just playing around, and everything calmed down.

I was really confused, I didn't know if they were playing or not, but I do know that the person that grabbed me knew I could have hurt him if I had intended. I went on to my cell and came back out to shower, wondering about the whole incident and if I had done wrong by striking someone. Even though it was not in anger and totally instinctive I felt like I had not reacted as a Christian. I was up most of the night wondering if there was another course of action I should have taken, and if I had caused any separation between the Lord and me. I prayed and asked the Lord for forgiveness if I had truly sinned and felt relieved.

I was feeling so much different now than when I first arrived, the Lord was truly transforming me, seemingly without me knowing it. I was constantly asking the Lord to create in me a clean heart and renew the right spirit within me, and never knew it was happening until circumstances reminded me of my previous thoughts and actions.

Chapter 18

FEELINGS

FEELING SICK AGAIN

The closer it got to the holidays the sicker I would get, a sinking feeling in the pit of my stomach stayed with me for months. My family was always on my mind regardless of what was happening around me. One other thing that always bothered me was that guards would say things like we should be happy that we don't have to pay any bills and get three square meals a day and recreation. They said it was more like a Holiday Inn than a prison. I couldn't speak for anyone else but I would have rather been a free dog than an imprisoned man.

This place or any prison will never take the place of home no matter how pleasant it appeared to people that could leave everyday.

I tried desperately to get transferred to "The Farm" it's the next step to being free with no barbed wire on the fences. According to the law they were not allowing armed robbers, murderers, and rapist to go, because their crimes represented all that was violent in nature. I would pray constantly for some type of relief. The warden was from hell and was changing everything, he was making it difficult for everyone even the guards. Visitation was becoming a nightmare, it seemed like he was trying to discourage inmates from even having visits, by making it so difficult for the visitors and us.

According to my paperwork I still had about two years to go and I couldn't imagine doing it there. Another inmate and I prayed everyday that the laws would change for us or the doors would open for us here, I was ready for a change, freedom would be greatly appreciated. We would settle for "The Farm" if we had to but deliver us from the belly of this beast.

THE WARDEN FROM HELL

The warden was threatening to take all our privileges; he had already stopped the visits on the picnic area and seemed to be always on the warpath. I figured he must have been insecure because he was so short, and had to make his presence seen. Whatever the case was, he seemed to have a big chip on his shoulder and took it out on inmates and the guards.

I just prayed harder and fasted, which really helped me out a great deal. The longest I had ever fasted was three days without food or water; it was a real spiritual experience. I was becoming weary of the spirit of hostility that hovered around us everyday, and it was starting to effect us all.

GOD CHANGED THE LAWS

March 1986 two years of incarceration, how have I made it through this and how has Deborah kept coming to visit me week after week, it has to be by the grace of God. By His grace I'm still maintaining and by His Grace I still have a hope of better days.

One very pleasant spring day my counselor brought me a paper from the department of corrections that indicated the change in the laws that would permit armed robbers to be eligible for consideration for community security. I kept reading, I couldn't understand what it was saying at first, but on the third or fourth time reading it I realized that it was saying that I could go to "The Farm" if the warden agreed.

I felt like I had made parole, I can leave here, I know this was the result of prayer, no one could make me believe that the Lord hadn't done this. I ran and showed it to my prayer partner and we had praise service right there. The Lord changed the laws for us, how great He is and worthy of all praise!

As the Lord would have it, I was the first of the armed robbers to be considered, and I was thrilled, but nervous. I told Deborah that I was going to "The Farm" but I didn't know when, this time we would be prepared and not get caught off guard. When the assistant supervisor realized I was leaving he was very emotional and called me the most honest and religious man he had known. I almost cried also because I never knew he felt that way. I was pleased.

THE TIMING MUST BE RIGHT

One thing I was concerned about was how would I deal with the fact that there was no escape prevention. With my strong desire to go home, will I be able to stay there for two more years, and what would happen if I had a bad dream, would I run?

I hated being locked up with a passion, but I will at least have a small taste of freedom, that should take some of the sting from the beast.

It was very apparent that something terrible was about to happen here, this warden had been transferred from another prison where a riot broke out, and understandably so. He was evil and seemed to purposely cause problems. He seemed pleased when visitors stopped coming, which caused hostility in the inmates. As a result of the lack of visits fights would break out, and these fights were different from the earlier ones, these were almost to the death.

When a fight broke out I would go in my cell and pray. On one occasion, a Puerto Rican friend of mine who was extremely cocky and very familiar with some kind of military self defense, which he used when his mouth got him into confrontations.

He and I would spar every now and then when no one was looking. Some of the other inmates were looking for an opportunity to hurt him; others were a little intimidated by his ability. This particular day somebody started a rumor that he was the one that snitched on the guys that tried to escape the other day. Their intentions were to get enough inmates mad enough so that more would jump him than he could handle. Some how he got wind of it, I think his cellmate told him. He threw open his cell door, started cracking his knuckles, and challenged the entire unit.

I started calling on the name of Jesus, and rebuking the devil, I was staring him down saying, "Jesus, Jesus, Jesus" it wasn't loud but audible. A few seconds went by, nobody moved; finally he turned and went back inside his cell. Everything continued as it had, no one said anything else about him being a snitch.

I don't want to think about what would have happened if the Lord hadn't intervened in that situation. It appeared, as though the design of the system was to cause havoc and mayhem, and the warden was there to secure the purpose.

It seemed like discouraging visitation wasn't enough, he introduced strip-searching to a lot of us who had never experienced it, and it was totally humiliating.

The reclassification to "The Farm" was a most welcome move on my part because I couldn't help but began to be very bitter about my life being wasted away. I had always felt that there was a certain amount of time an inmate could spend in prison and he would never return, but beyond that he is sure to repeat. Even with all the blessings I could see, I could tell that this place was having a very negative influence on my mind. I kept thinking that if the Public Defender that represented me at the beginning, the DA, and the Detective for the Public Defender's office hadn't lied about the identification, I wouldn't be here suffering as I was.

I was glad to be leaving I hoped in another place the Lord can help me get rid of some of this hatred I had for them and the need for vengeance I felt.

FEELING STRANGE ABOUT LEAVING

The day I left there caused a strange feeling to come over me, I was happy to be leaving but would have rather been going home instead of another prison. Packing all my stuff felt good but to a bitter beat because I knew that my freedom from prison was still in a distant time.

I arrived at "The Farm" in May 1986, it was a beautiful day, but I still had this sick feeling, I just missed my family, and wanted to be home with them. I believe I was the only one that was transferred that day, but I do know I was the first armed robber that left from there.

I swallowed the going home notion, and pretended to have strength as I had been doing. Seeing some of my old friends there that had gone before me made me feel like I was an old head in the system, and I didn't like that at all. This time, coming in to a new facility wasn't as hard; everyone knew that I had to have come from some prison before I came there.

I could see the handy work of the Lord working in my life up to now, but I couldn't understand why I was still incarcerated. How much more did I have to endure? What was the Lord doing, keeping me here until my marriage ended, or until I lost my mind? Sometimes I felt like God was punishing me for the extremely sinful life I'd lived before I came.

I stayed sick on the inside as I went through the motions of getting checked in and being assigned a unit. I tried hard to shake off thoughts of being with Deborah, but the harder I tried the stronger the thoughts would come. I guess it being the cool of the day made me even more homesick.

By the time I got down to the unit, I was starting to get a little nervous; this place was more like an army camp. Each unit had one big open space for beds where we slept. Each inmate had their own headboard for personals and a tall standup cabinet for clothes and other items. It was completely different from the other place, not to mention the fact that there were no razor wires on the fence. The gate was opened all day, with an unarmed guard inside a little shack.

The place was wide opened, it seemed that inmates could do whatever they wanted, and I didn't know whether this was a good place or not. It would take an extremely strong individual to stay here and not get caught up in the looseness. A person could easily fall victim to the web caused by the semi-freedom, and resort back to his criminal ways and get shipped out in chains.

The carrot dangling on a pole, so close but yet so far, free but unable to leave, what a concept. I still have to spend lonely nights in a crowded room with men that don't seem to mind where they are. One thing about it, it seemed like these guys were friendlier and more willing to help, now that was odd.

MORE DISCOMFORTING FEELINGS

A little over two years now, and I still am not comfortable having to deal with my wife out there without me, living her life absent of the protection and support I'm suppose to give her. It's still hard to deal with the fact that they felt like I needed to be off the streets, and sent me to prison and wouldn't give me any kind of break at all, when it came to my freedom. God help me not to hate. I don't belong in this man's prison. Does anybody even care that I'm not the same young fool that I once was, that I'm not a threat to society? Does anybody care that I have a family out there that I need and that need me? I guess not, I'm still here.

Someone is already asking me if I need any weed, or whisky or anything else, cause if I need it they know where to find it. "No I don't do any of those things, I 'm trying hard to get out, and stay out.

The first weekend I was there was like a wild party on the streets, every body seemed to be either drunk or high, some even climbed over the fence, but came back later before count. If there was anything I was tempted to do, that was it. My mind started changing after a few weekends, those guys were not getting caught, and it seemed like they were not having as hard as time as I was. I thought maybe if I just got a little buzz, maybe I could cope a little better. I wrestled with those thoughts for weeks, but realized that the Lord had not brought me this far to leave me. I started praying more in tongues, reading the Bible more and fasting, stirring up the Spirit in me. Before long greater was He that was in me, than he that was in the world.

Thank the Lord I never did any of those things, for had I begun I never would have stopped.

Chapter 19

THE FARM & FREEDOM EXPERIENCE

"THE FARM"

Everybody worked at "The Farm", and before they found you a job you worked on the "Long Line", a long line of inmates working like a chain gang, without the chain. Every morning a guard would start yelling, "long line, long line," and those inmates that didn't have a job would follow him. I really didn't want to work on a line chopping down weeds, and cutting grass on the streets, not that I thought I was too good for that but it wasn't going to benefit me any. I wanted to do something that was going to help me when I got out, although I had no idea what was there for me to do.

Again I cried unto the Lord, and he heard me. The man over the recreation area had gone to TSU when I had attended there and had also seen me perform as a comic. He got me a job in the rec room, cleaning the weight room and the recreation area. It was not what I wanted, but it kept me from working on the "Long Line."

HAVING THE FAVOR OF GOD

I had only worked there for a few weeks when a black female guard asked me if I'd like to work in her office typing daily inmate records concerning job placements. I had no prior typing experience, and I told her, but she allowed me to keep the job because she liked my attitude. I knew it was the Lord, how could she like my attitude if I had never talked to her? This was amazing, I had my own desk, inside an air-condition building, doing something I had never done before. What a mighty God I serve!

I did not apply for the job nor did I know the job existed, but once again I was accused of being a snitch because others had wanted the job, and had been there a lot longer than I. Most of the inmates stayed away from me because I didn't participate in the activities they participated in. No one dared call me a snitch to my face, I would overhear it said as I was walking by, or they would stop talking after seeing me walk up. It really didn't bother me; I was too busy thinking about leaving, and besides they would see me talking to some of the so called tough guys, who were friends that were with me at the other prison, I think they were a little nervous about saying anything out of the way to me.

I really had no fear of anyone and I guess I had always displayed that kind of air, not cocky, just not scared. I felt like God had protected me this far and as long as I stayed right He would always keep His angels around me.

The work place seemed to draw almost every administrator in the institution at one time or another, even the warden and the assistant warden, who both happened to be black. My experience with blacks in the correction systems caused me to keep my distance from them, especially because I too was black.

I did the job as effective as I could, most of the administrators would come by and talk, I didn't talk unless it was totally necessary, and it was always to aid in some way. The main thing that stayed on my mind was that I wished I were going home this evening, instead of to a building full of men.

I was able to know every job on the compound and how many workers were allowed on the job. There was a program called Level Two, a program allowing inmates that were not eligible for work release to work outside the institution on a regular type job.

Most of them were janitorial jobs, but there was one that was in an office doing data entry, only two inmates allowed to occupy. When I realized an opening in the data entry position downtown became available, I mentioned to myself "if I were to go to a Level Two job this one would be the one I'd want." This was said only in my mind.

IT BEGAN WITH A THOUGHT

After about a month of feeling like a zombie, walking around as if I was not being affected by the semi-freedom I was experiencing, the Assistant Warden noticed my name on the Level Two roster, told me he had the perfect job for me. I had never said anything to him about the job but it was the exact job I had wanted. Again it just blew my mind how things like this were happening but the prayers for my freedom were going unanswered.

I didn't know whether I was ready for a Level Two job, when I left this prison I want to be going home, not to return. I was sick, I just couldn't seem to relax incarcerated knowing I just recently witnessed my 4th year wedding anniversary passing by like just another day. I had always toyed with women's emotions and had strong feelings for only myself and never knew what it could be like to love. When I finally found it I was carted off like a crazed criminal.

Sometimes the anger and hatred would try to creep back in as I wandered around the compound at night feeling totally isolated not only from the outside world but from the inside as well. Trapped from within and trapped from without having to suppress my inward feelings and unable to leave a place with no barbed or razor wire, and where the gate is open all day. I wasn't anxious about going downtown so I didn't make any effort to rush the procedures.

A NEW EXPERIENCE

I had become acquainted with the free world personnel where I was currently working but it was hard watching inmates go home almost every day. Working around them everyday made it a little easier to deal with them, plus they were not as prideful acting as the other personnel at the other institution. They treated me more like a person and not a number or a criminal so I was a little more relaxed around them but as always I remained disciplined not letting down walls I had built up.

What a psychological game, opened gate, no barbed wire, people treating you almost human, but you can't go home. The temptation was not as controlled by some as others. Some did escape and they only had a small amount of time left to do. What made that so scary to me is that I understood exactly how they felt. The thing I longed for, for almost 2 ½ years was now at my fingertip, I could taste freedom, but they were now holding me by an invisible fence, and I can leave if I want to, but then what?

I had to take a deep breath, shake my head and keep waking up every morning until it ended. According to my paperwork I still had at least 3 more years to do before I'm eligible for a parole hearing. I just didn't know how I could do it.

It is easy to perform a good action, but not easy to acquire a settled habit of performing such actions.

Aristotle

Chapter 20

DOWNTOWN

STILL QUESTIONING GOD

Sometimes it seemed like God was nowhere around, but when I stopped to think about it God had been with me from day one. I knew the Lord was in this with me but how long would I have to be punished for the sins I had committed in the past? I guess the thing that bothered me the most was, how long before Deborah decides enough is enough and stopped seeing me and called off the marriage. I knew she had gotten saved but I also knew she was human. She, just as I, had human needs and desires. Sometimes my thoughts would overwhelm me and I would get sick and want to yell, but every time I looked around, most of the other men didn't seem to care where they were, so I held in my scream.

It's almost as if I had started all over again, a new place, new people but still can't go home. Maybe I should have stayed where I was until I was free altogether. I really didn't know if I could deal with this. Doing time was not something I could ever get used to, no matter what kind of place they put me in.

THE VISIT DOWNTOWN

Deborah had to bring all my clothes to me; I had to wear a tie at the job downtown. It had been a while since I had on "real" clothes and the morning I was to report to the downtown job my eyes filled with tears and a lump developed in my throat, I almost looked human.

The day I went downtown another inmate went with me. He was a white man, very smart and highly talkative. He had a resume and everything I had nothing but myself and didn't really say much at the interview with the employers at the downtown office. I got the job, the same one I thought about. He didn't get that job but another one on the Level Two and escaped one day after only a few days of work.

I was in the office with the workers in a State department. It seemed as though they had helped another inmate keep that job when he got out and another inmate worked there who had only a few months to go.

CONCERNED ABOUT TEMPTATION

I had been locked up for a little over 2 ½ years and I was very much concerned about my previous problems with attractive women and the fact that women had always seemed to be available to me, whether I was looking or not. Since my marriage, Deborah had gotten my full attention and love, but now I'm almost like a hungry lion on the inside that hadn't had anything to eat for years. My determination to stay saved was now being threatened. I knew that I could keep from coming on to them but what about their advances?

SAMPSON'S WEAKNESS REVEALED

At the moment I actually knew I was going downtown I got concerned about my ability to maintain myself. I prayed desperately about that situation. I guess I could have just not accepted the job, but I felt that God had opened that door and I didn't want to miss out on any blessings. In my time of praying the Lord allowed the story of Sampson to come across my mind. I read it but didn't understand it's meaning. I kept reading the story and finally realized that all the power he had, he still had a problem with his eyes. As soon as I began to realize that, the Lord began to open up certain keys to me about keeping myself clean in an unclean world. I had to carry myself in a way that women would respect my stand concerning faithfulness and my relationship with God.

THE KEY

If things ever were to seem out of hand in our conversations my speaking of the things of God always makes the difference. I had to control what I looked at and how long I looked. The eyes were the gateway to the mind, so if I were to see something that could cause me problems I would simply look off.

The key wasn't easy at first but after practicing, it became second nature because I realized if a person wants to be kept, the God in them was willing to help. I was getting more and more evidence that the Holy Ghost is the power if we would first get it and use it. It was not easy but God was helping me every step of the way.

The job was extremely boring, I had my own desk, my own phone and I was free to go to lunch alone for an hour without any guard following me around. As a matter of fact I had no supervision from the prison the entire time I got off the van until they picked me up that evening.

Chapter 21

RENDEZVOUS

VISITATION AT THE FARM

Visitation at the farm was different from that at the Reception Center. Whatever you could imagine out on the visiting yard was happening. At one time it was wide-open sex and touching all around us. I had too much respect for Deborah to even think about suggesting things of that nature, but deep down inside I deeply desired to be intimate with her. It was good for me that they cracked down on the things that were happening there. Neither of us were very sure of how much more control we could use with all that was happening around us.

THE STRUGGLES WITHIN

I would struggle within myself everyday, building up myself spiritually, mentally and emotionally. The temptation to escape or to take some of the women up on their advances was always present. Although the men on the job thought I was gay or not bothered by the females around us, only I knew how much fighting I did within and how I constantly prayed that I would stay faithful to God and my wife. It got so very difficult that I almost decided to stop the job and return to work at the compound. On the day I had made my mind up to quit, the man over my job came to me and told me that if I wanted one day, I could leave at lunch as long as I made sure I was at the van at the end of the day. That was enough for me, I didn't question him or God, I just called Deborah and relayed the information to her. It was like I told her I was going to be released.

The idea of inquiring from God concerning this matter was unreasonable. Why should I ask God something I know is wrong and totally fleshly?

With all the right I was so desperately striving to pursue, an opportunity to spend some unsupervised time with my wife was a deed I didn't even attempt to resist. I guess I rationalized it to be all right with God since it was my wife, and not the women on the job who were so available. Whatever the Holy Ghost might have said was smothered out by my strong desire to be with Deborah. If the guards didn't catch me, I felt that God's mercy endured forever.

THE PLANS TO RENDEZVOUS

We had set a date where it would be convenient for her, which was about 2 weeks off, and during those weeks our conversation changed. All we talked about was being able to be together unsupervised for at least 4 hours. I couldn't sleep at night and was totally unable to concentrate on my job. It was hard not running around the compound telling everyone what I was looking forward to but I knew I had to keep it quiet.

I guess I should have thought about how much trouble I could have gotten into but I didn't. I had tunnel vision and the only thing on my mind was Deborah, and being able to be with her. The closer it got to the end of the two weeks the more nervous I became. I didn't want to act like a raving maniac, like I really felt; I wanted to maintain discipline and self-control.

DRIVEN LIKE A WILD ANIMAL

The morning of the rendezvous seemed to take forever getting there and the hours till 12:00 noon seemed even longer. By the time 12:00 had gotten there I was so nervous I was sweating like a wild boar, it seemed like I was going to pass out. The walk to the hotel was a little frightening, I felt like everyone on the street knew what I was doing and that maybe today the guards would come downtown to visit inmates on their jobs.

Although I was extremely paranoid the human nature inside me drove me like a madman. The closer I got to her hotel room the more the reality hit me that it was really happening. Seeing her and knowing that there were no restraints made all the paranoia and the nervousness cease.

The drive back to the compound that evening was a blur and I'm sure I had a far off look on my face. Being able to be with Deborah made things for me a lot easier on the job, but it increased my anxiety to go home. The expression of love was more than physical it was emotional as well.

Chapter 22

THE DANGLING CARROT

THE SAFTY VALVE

The prisons were constantly overcrowded and they had developed what they referred to as a safety valve, which gave inmates an opportunity to meet the parole board earlier than anticipated. After finding out how they calculated time I added up mine and realized that I should be meeting the parole board a lot sooner than expected, maybe even this year.

I didn't want to get my hopes up, I'd been disappointed with the system for so long I wasn't' about to start believing in it again. I went to see my counselor to get some information and to my surprise he had already calculated when I should meet the parole board. He said, "if the overcrowding continues and the safety valve is still in effect, you should be eligible by February or March of next year". That wasn't what I was hoping for but at least I had something to look forward to. It wasn't as close as I had wanted, but it's closer than my original papers and for that I thanked God. This was surely the most comforting news we had heard in a long time, at last a break, something to see, a hope.

MY STANDARD ROUTINE

I didn't fellowship with hardly any of the inmates there. I had a routine I stuck to everyday. After work I'd change clothes go to the weight room until suppertime. I'd eat and go to the unit, shower, read the Bible, watch a little T.V., talk to Deborah on the phone and go to bed. Saturdays were usually visiting day and Sundays were long days.

ANOTHER CLOSE CALL

I had played a little basketball but I had to quit because I came close to fighting one day. There was a young man about 21 years old, thin but tall about 6 feet 2 inches, extremely cocky and had a foul mouth. I had played ball with some rough characters, a lot tougher than these guys were but it seemed as though they were always trying to prove to someone how tough they were.

This guy would always try to run over guys smaller than he was to get a lay-up or dunk. I would simply shift my body to the side and strip the ball from him. He was yelling and swearing that I'd fouled him and that he was going to knock me out it I fouled him again. I should have just walked off the court but I got a little upset at him and was really tempted to hit him purposely.

I knew the next time he got the ball he was going to try and run into me; so when he came charging to the goal I didn't try to steal the ball, I waited until he almost bumped me and I shifted my body and he fell hard to the ground. He jumped up swearing and threatening, some of them grabbed him before he got to me. He was spewing out threats and calling me names, I wanted so bad to tell them to please let him go. The anger he had could easily be used against him.

He was about a kick's length away from me, I didn't say a word, I looked at him slightly smiling and walked off the court. He yelled names and threats until I had gotten out of sight. With every step I took and every name he called me there was a war not to go back and really show him how much of a punk I really was.

THE BEATING I WANTED TO GIVE

When I saw that young man the next day he looked like someone had stayed up all night beating him. Someone on the basketball court gave him the whipping I wanted to give him; of course he couldn't look me in the eye. I just looked at him and said, "what's up?" I'm sure the reason he didn't speak back was because his mouth was hurting too bad. After that incident I didn't go back to the basketball court.

What always amazed me was you could do all the right things fast, pray, read and watch, but the devil would jump in at any given time he has an opportunity and it didn't take but a second. The carrot was now dangling before me, a parole hearing on the horizon; time now to be more cautious than ever. I've witnessed inmates days before their release date get in trouble, go back to court and get more time. It seemed like a work of Satan to keep men locked up away from society.

THE TRICK OF THE DEVIL

Satan worked in other inmates to cause them problems and lose their temper, hurt and even kill someone. Some would after making parole come in from work drunk or strung out on drugs and lose their parole and have to wait for their regular date. They didn't seem to understand that this was an early parole date, if they gave it to you, they could take it away.

Just knowing I was getting close, gave me a sense of relief in a way that made me not want to take anything off anyone, even the guards. It was harder than ever not to say something smart to them. It seemed as though my guards were being slowly let down, I was easily falling in the same trap as others. I had to really back up and start fasting again to get my flesh back under control. It was a scary time, I had only been told that I had an early parole date and already I was battling with myself. I understood completely how the other inmates could get caught up and loose it.

Chapter 23

SEARCH FOR TOMORROW

LEANING ON THE LORD

I had to strongly lean on the Holy Ghost to help me to stay sane because on the other side of the coin there was fear creeping in. What if I didn't make parole even after I came up for it? There were a lot of inmates going up for parole but not all were getting out. It was even rumored that no armed robbers, rapist, or murders were being released early.

I would only be discouraged for a little while until I realized how God had been with me from the beginning. I knew that my situation, though similar, was different in the eyes of God. I'd watched others get turned down and rationalized why I felt that they didn't make it, but it all boiled down to the fact that they themselves were not in charge of their lives. There was another force ruling the outcome. I had to rely on the same help that has been there for me all along. I had to stay in the blessing position; I had to keep my heart right, not just go through the motions.

If all goes well, the day I've been looking for from the beginning, was slowly coming to past. Even though there was a sense of joy inside me, I wanted to be careful not to be overwhelmed, because things of this nature sometimes caused envy in the hearts of others that were not close to their dates. Envy stirred up strife and fights would break out. Men were being shipped back to the other institution everyday because of misconduct.

I didn't go around telling anyone about my possible early parole I really didn't need anymore trouble than I was already getting. There were some guards that were over friendly and some were just mean, black and white. I tried hard to just stay away from them all. One guard told me "nobody can be this good, you must be doing something", so I figured I'd better stop my meetings with Deborah to avoid any problems, but it was good while it lasted.

A DIFFERENT HOLIDAY SPIRIT

The 1986 Holiday season was not quite as difficult as the others. I had a strange feeling that this would be Deborah's last birthday, Thanksgiving, Christmas, and Wedding Anniversary that I would spend away from home. During visitation we would have mixed emotions, some joy and anxiousness, joyous with hope of freedom and anxiousness because we were tired.

Working downtown really helped with the holiday blues. I had an out, a way to escape from the system for at least 8 hours. Incidentally one day on my way to lunch, that guard that warned me about me doing something, followed me. I had seen him from the window up on the 5th floor of my job and knew where he was and what he was wearing. I was watching him follow me from the reflections in some of the buildings. When I got in a crowd of people I hid myself and watched him pass me looking like Barney Fife, wondering where I had gone.

Somehow it seemed like the crowd opened up and he was looking all around for me as I walked up from behind him. He was almost standing in the middle of the sidewalk and was looking behind him when he saw me. I didn't smile or change my expressions I just looked at him up and down and was almost walking backwards watching him with that surprised look on his face. When I would see him on the compound afterwards he would always look at me with that "you think you're smart don't you" look. I would just look at him with no expression at all.

Staying busy made the holiday season pass with a little more ease than ever before. This was my third season and I don't know how I could have made it if God had not been with me. There seemed to be a spirit about Christmas that causes me to have this strange longing feeling in the pit of my stomach. I wanted so much to be home enjoying all the holiday activities that I had taken for granted in time past. I tried to believe that by next year this time for sure I'd be home.

ANOTHER WEDDING ANNIVERSARY

January 1st 1987 my 5th year wedding anniversary with these last 3 years spent away from the woman I love. I did what I normally would do; I sent her a card and tried to assure her of what I was trying to assure myself of that we would celebrate our 6th year together.

I was glad all the days off from work were over because all I did on the compound was to think. One positive thing was that I was able to read and study quite a bit from the Bible, which kept me motivated. The Pastor from my wife's church, the same man that married us in 1982 was coming out to see me regularly, he became a good friend. He was an easy person to talk to and I was able to freely tell him all that was in my heart, something I had never been able to do. We always prayed that I would go up for parole earlier than my papers indicated and last I checked I should go up in March. If I were to go up for parole in March I should be home by summer.

FIGHTING MORE DESIRES

I was like a man experiencing love for the first time, I longed to spend another evening with Deborah but I dare not for the risk was too high. Something had to happen, I knew I was close, but my desires were overwhelming my mind. I believed that if I had called her, Deborah would have come downtown again to meet me but I fought hard not to ask her. I would sleep at night curled up in a ball to ease the pain in my stomach.

AN ON TIME FURLOUGH

One day I went to work my sister called me and told me my father was admitted to the hospital. His hospital visit was a blessing in disguise. Because my parole date was close I was allowed to have a 3-day emergency furlough, it came just like that. They checked the hospital and sent me on my way. The only requirement was to check with the Sheriff's department in Jackson when I got there and to be back on time after 3 days.

I absolutely could not believe I was actually leaving for 3 days. Deborah came and picked me up and let me drive. I had not forgotten how even though I thought I had. Since it was late evening when we left the prison we didn't leave for Jackson until morning. By the time we got to Jackson my dad was out of the hospital and it was like a family reunion. It was a great time even though my mom and dad were divorced it was a refreshing blessing being around the family with my family.

It was a glorious 3 days and I was quite sad to have to go back. I felt like it was so unnecessary for me to go back to prison seeing that my total desire is to be back with my family. I sucked it in and tried to pretend that I was okay with it. I got to the compound and caught a ride downtown to work; I just didn't want to hang around there. I wasn't ready for the incarcerated feeling just yet. It took me a few days to recuperate from those 3 days. If they could let me out on a furlough why couldn't they just let me go?

They didn't really know "how" much I was paying for the crimes I had committed in the past. Every aspect of this incarceration has tormented me in one-way or the other. I thanked God for the furlough but wondered why I had to come back. I guess they were testing me to see what was really in me, I guess. I knew God knew me and I hoped He knew what was best for me.

GOOD NEWS AT THE LAST MINUTE

I was sitting on my bunk after supper one evening counting the days until March. I had my head in my hand and sighed. One of my friends came running in and told me that my name was on the parole docket for January. "January?" I jumped up and ran over to operations with my mouth wide opened. I saw my name...I almost passed out! My eyes filled up with tears but I sucked them back in and ran outside. Once outside tears started streaming down and I couldn't stop them. It was already dark outside and cold but I stayed out until I got myself together. Those that were outside probably thought I was crazy pacing back and forth praising God in the cold darkness. I went inside and wanted to call Deborah but every time I thought I should call, a lump would come in my throat and I felt like I was going to be crying on the phone.

When I got to work the next morning I called Deborah and calmly told her that I was on the docket for January. She silently screamed if there is such a thing and we rejoiced together for a while on the phone. She and I called friends who we wanted to be there for us at the hearing. It was only a week's notice but everyone was pleased to be a part of the hearing. One of the supervisors on my job insisted that he would be there also. I was in shock as to how soon things seemed to be happening. "Thank you Lord" was all I could say all daylong everyday.

THE PAROLE HEARING

On the morning of the parole hearing I was dressed in my work clothes, I was going to work afterwards regardless of the outcome. I was nervous but confident that God was in control. There were a great number of people there to support me, even my friend that was locked up with me back in 1984 who had helped me out spiritually. The preacher that baptized me, my wife's pastor, my sisters and my wife were there to support as well.

When I went in the hearing room I could feel my heart beating and my shallow breathing. No armed robbers were being released but I was no longer an armed robber. I'm now a son, and God was now in charge of my life.

There were two white males and one white female who was the institutional parole officer and was on the compound daily, who I had never said one word to. They didn't even look at me; they turned on a recorder, had everyone introduce him or herself and asked me about what happened eight years ago at the car wash in June. I rehearsed the incident from beginning to end and stopped. "In June 1979, a friend and I had been drinking and smoking marijuana, we started driving around looking for a potential victim and spotted a lady at a carwash, I drove up, got out of the car, held the pistol on her and demanded her money, she gave it to me, I got back in the car and drove off." The two men were like angry dogs, they spewed questions about the incident and I calmly answered. Right in the middle of them asking questions the female said, "he has already been to trial and he's admitted to his guilt, I'm voting to release him. I know him, he's a good person and he has never caused any problems." The men looked at her and also voted to recommend parole, and said "good day Mr. Walton", still not looking at me.

All of us were praising God and hugging, it was a joyous occasion. They recommended me to go to my parole date, which was May 29th. I had a date, May 29th, it's not today but it is this year. I can handle that, I guess. That day I was the only one that made parole and the first armed robber in a while.

I caught a ride to work and was in a daze all the rest of that day. I tried not to be happy around the other inmates as to not hurt their feelings because I was leaving soon and they weren't. Regardless of how happy we were when someone was leaving we always had a deep desire that it was us along with them or instead of them. When they would ask me if I made it, I would just tell them "so far but we never know until we walk out."

Chapter 24

BEGINNING OF THE END

IT'S ALMOST OVER

Deborah's and my conversations changed almost overnight, joy and a hope at last were in sight. I couldn't believe it; the nightmare was almost over, a few more months. I had not long come from a 3-day furlough that helped tremendously. I can do 4 months standing in a corner.

In February, about 3 weeks after my hearing there came a response from downtown concern my hearing. The main Parole Board approved everything. I was set. It was up to me now to make sure I remained true to God that He may continue with His blessings.

Working and working out helped to make time pass by a lot sooner. It was all I could do to keep from skipping around the compound like a kid.

THREE CALENDER YEARS

March 7, 1987 I've been locked up now for 3 years. I pondered over the thought of how in the world I survived with my senses intact and how I was kept under the shadow of the Almighty the entire time; from the desire to kill myself, and the trance I was in then, up to now. Seeing the hand of God and realizing that things could have been so much worse, and that if it had not been for the Lord, these last 3 years could have been more of a nightmare than it was.

It didn't seem totally real; I kept expecting something else to happen to change their minds. I was still somewhat cautious because I was still there and I still was not totally relaxed in the decision of the board. As far as my freedom was concerned nothing positive had happened in almost 3 years and all of a sudden I'm facing freedom in a way and manner I'd not faced before.

IT'S HARD TO CONCENTRATE

It was not easy to believe the things that were happening during this time. They were coming to me telling me when my "out-date" was and that I could get another furlough in May. In April my wife got a call from the supervisor of the grocery store I had worked in before prison. They wondered when I was getting out. They told her as soon as I was released they had a job for me. Although I used them as my job reference to make parole I had not officially asked them but I felt like they would rehire me.

It was very difficult to concentrate on the job and to maintain my regular schedule. I tried hard to just keep doing what I had been doing for the past year but I couldn't help but think this could finally be over. I kept thinking that one day soon I'd be leaving this place not to ever return again, Thank God! Most of the prayers I'd ever prayed in prison had been answered except the one concerning my freedom and now the answer to that prayer was on the horizon.

ANOTHER FURLOUGH

According to my parole papers my "out-date" was May 29th, it's now May and the days started slowing down, thank God for a furlough scheduled for the 10th, a Sunday. Deborah came and picked me up on Sunday morning, we spend the day in church and Monday & Tuesday we spent together, Wednesday I had to be back by noon. Wednesday about 11:00am my wife and I, the Pastor and my sister met at church and prayed. I was really frustrated at the fact that I had to go back. I was asking God to please fix it some way that I wouldn't have to stay until the 29th. I don't know how, but I know you are able. It just didn't make any sense for me to remain there anymore I was really tired.

You can't separate peace from freedom because no one can be at peace unless he has his freedom.

Malcolm X (1925 -1965), Malcolm X Speaks, 1965

Chapter 25

LONG TIME COMING

THE LAST DAY

I got back to the compound about noon and asked if someone could take me in to work. I wanted to be on the compound as little as possible. I took my clothes and put them up and came back outside to wait for someone to become available to take me to work. I guess I should have been glad I had a chance to go home and glad I had only a few more days but I wanted to go now.

I rode to work looking out the window reminiscing about the past 3 days. I put on a happy face when I got to my floor and everyone was smiling and glad to see me as usual, but this time was a little different. Between the time I got out of the van and I got up to my work place someone had called from the compound to tell them that my parole certificate was there, my time was up, I can go home,...... I am free!

I flopped down in a chair and almost burst into tears of joy, but I stood up quickly, called my wife at her job left her a message to come back and get me. I called back to the compound and found out that someone I had befriended when I worked in that office had made special efforts to get my paper from the parole office before I returned from furlough and the paper had just arrived. They had also contacted the officer who dropped me off to turn around to pick me back up. I hugged everyone in the office, the females cried and the men were teary eyed, I was just smiling hard. The van couldn't get back to the compound soon enough. I jumped out and ran up to the unit.

Deborah was already there when I got finished packing. I left a lot of things I just didn't care, I wanted out. May 13, 1987 I walked out of prison a free man. Everything happened so fast I didn't get a chance to think about the fact that it was finally over.

FREEDOM

It was Wednesday when I left The Farm and it felt good! The feeling of freedom was indescribable. I've survived and waited for this particular day a long time. The weather was perfect and the drive home was extraordinary. I didn't tell Deborah until later what the guard said about me coming back, because they all come back sooner or later. I was too busy being happy to comment so I kept walking.

Deborah and Jaimee were still staying with her brother so that was home for me as well. Wednesday night Bible Class and Sunday Service were totally awesome! I testified that night and felt good about it. All I could do was smile, and think to myself, "God is so good."

Monday I was working sacking groceries at Compton's Foodland, I'm sure I was the happiest bagger in the whole store, and probably the oldest, but it didn't matter.

I didn't have a vehicle at the time so I walked sometimes and Deborah picked me up or I got a ride with someone. God always worked it out.

After a while of living with no vehicle, I remembered what I would confess to the other inmates when I would see one of those trucks on our way to the job site. I kept saying that I was going to get one of those trucks when I get out.

I decided to go to the Toyota place. I picked out a truck, laid hands on it and went to the salesman. I told him where I had been and what I needed. He looked at me strange, appreciated my honesty and said he'd see what he could do. A few days later Deborah was able to go pick it up and drop it off at my job.

The truck was a five-speed. We could hardly drive it but we managed and I had a totally new Toyota pick-up truck in just a few months out of prison. I kept seeing God in every turn.

The next thing we needed was a house of our own. We obtained a realtor, found a house, laid hands on it and were able to purchase it, even with my prison record.

In less than six months out of prison, God had blessed us with a new truck and our very own first home.

STILL HAVING TO FIGHT

The first year of freedom was a very difficult year for me, trying to adjust to this new life. Even though the Lord was Blessing us, the devil was also kicking up a lot of dirt as well. Somehow some of my old friends popped up out of nowhere and tried hard to pull me back into the person they knew from the past.

Freedom has a price, it can if you let it, make you take it for granted and almost forget the years you spent crying for it. Sometimes the thing you press so hard to obtain ends up not being as pleasant as you had hoped. Responsibility is a powerful drive to either do the right thing or the wrong to fulfill it.

A committed heart and the Power of the Holy Ghost kept me focused on doing the right thing. Some days were harder than others, because I had lived worldly longer than I had lived for God. Sometimes my short experience with God seemed no match with the longtime relationship I had with the world, but God always showed up and helped me to do His will.

I eventually started working in the management program at the grocer, and that alone was a Blessing. I was the first Black person that the owner had ever had in a management position in the history of his company.

THE SET UP

Two years after I was released in 1989 Deborah gave birth to our first child together, Alexander Montrel Walton. With his birth I came face to face with a genuine total desire to be the best man, husband and father that God would give me the strength to be. It was that same year I "accepted my call to the ministry" and received courage to start a prison ministry. However, I didn't preach my first sermon until 1993.

In the process of time I became the manager of the store where I had started sacking groceries. I became totally responsible for the entire store. I was given the keys, the combination to the safe and the code to the security system. The Favor of God was all around me and I dared not to bring a reproach on His Holy Name. Thank God, there was never ever a desire to do any illegal activity as before. We purchased our second home shortly after I had become the Store Manager.

I was chosen to be on the Board of Directors at Greater Christ Temple Church and held many leadership positions under the tutelage of then, Elder Sherman Merritt who not only was my Pastor but a true friend.

I wrote several articles for The Tennessean newspaper without ever considering being a writer. God was setting me up to not be afraid to speak my mind on controversial topics in spite of the thoughts of people, if the motives were to set the captive free.

Elder Merritt became District Elder and he had the responsibility of selling a building that was once a bar in Paducah, KY. A minister from Louisville, KY had tried to build a work in it but was not successful. The building had lain dormant for a while and was causing The Kentucky and Tennessee Council money keeping the property up.

After several attempts to sell the building fell through, District Elder Merritt decided that Greater Christ Temple Church would purchase it. Personally I thought it was a bad idea because it was two hours away and it was a totally underdeveloped piece of property in a bad neighborhood.

STEPPING INTO DESTINY

I'll never forget I was driving Pastor Merritt to St Louis one day and we stopped in Paducah to check on the Brother who was working on preparing the building for Service. We offered to help with some of the painting. I was putting a coat of paint on the back wall with a roller and was thinking to myself, "What idiot is going to drive this far to start up a Church from the ground in this bad neighborhood?"

Christ Temple in Paducah, KY began Services in September 1998. Another Minister from our Church felt that God had called him to be the Pastor, so he started going up. The amazing thing about all this was that every time the Board brought up the Church, a sister sitting across from me would always point at me. I just thought she was nuts and just overlooked it.

My job, family and ministry responsibilities made it difficult to imagine myself doing anything other than what I was doing. Certainly Paducah, Kentucky was the last thing on my mind. However, after six months the minister who went to Paducah decided to let it be known on the first Sunday of April that this was going to be his last month.

I was waiting for someone else to step up and take the challenge, but no one did. Pastor Merritt was trying to determine how he was going to operate both places, because he was certain that the Church was a God move.

As a minister of the Church and a friend of the Pastor and my concern for him, I decided to take that burden off him by proclaiming my intentions. "I will go to Paducah until you find someone." I had already talked to the owner of the Grocery Store and my two Assistant Managers, and we came up with a plan that allowed me to be free from 8 to 5 on Sundays. I convinced them all that it would be for at least three months.

Needless to say the last Sunday in April 1998 began my journey; I was installed as the Pastor in 2000. I ended my job after 14 years in 2001 and moved to Paducah in 2005. God has shown His approval in so many ways. We ended up purchasing the whole block, and the Church has grown considerably.

Never before had I paid any attention to the number 7 on this Church journey until God revealed it to me recently:

From the year I started going to Paducah (98) until we actually moved there (05) = **7 years.**

From my Installation year (2000) until the steel building our Church is now in was donated to us (2007) = **7 years.**

From the time we moved to Paducah (2005) until the new Church was built (2012) = **7 years.**

There has to be more in my life somewhere, but those were revealed to me recently.

It's August 2014 at the present. Deborah and I have celebrated 32 years of marriage. Since my release in 1987 I've been totally committed to serving Jesus Christ.

Jaimee is married with children and so is Alexander who has been very instrumental with the ministry. Jaimee and my other son Anthony both live in Nashville while Alexander lives in Paducah. God has opened many doors for me here and I made a promise to Him that whatever door He opens, I'm stepping in.

The thought of those prison years still haunt me today. I still awake sometimes at night after having a nightmare, thanking God that I made it through the worst years of my life. I will never forget those years, how close I really came to death and how this terrible experience brought me to an indescribable relationship with God, which altered my life forever, for through it all, I thank God for continuing to keep me "Under The Shadow" of the Almighty.

Stay out of jail.
Alfred Hitchcock

GLOSSARY

1. **Adamant** - unshakable or immovable especially in opposition: unyielding.

2. **Agitate** - to excite and often trouble the mind or feelings of: disturb.

3. **Animalistic** – a natural unrestrained unreasoned response to physical drives or stimuli: the animal nature of human beings.

4. **Asphyxiating** - to cause asphyxia in; also: to kill or make unconscious by inadequate oxygen, presence of noxious agents, or other obstruction to normal breathing.

5. **Barbaric** - of, relating to, or characteristic of barbarians: possessing or characteristic of a cultural level more complex than primitive savagery but less sophisticated than advanced civilization.

6. **Despair** - utter loss of hope: a cause of hopelessness.

7. **Docket** - a formal abridged record of the proceedings in a legal action.

8. **Elate** - to fill with joy or pride: marked by high spirits.

9. **Exhort** - to incite by argument or advice: urge strongly: to give warnings or advice: make urgent appeals.

10. **Exit Inn** – a popular night club in Nashville, mostly popular for new talent.

11. **Free world**—anyone who worked or visited the prison who was not an inmate.

12. **Fort Pillow** - Fort Pillow Prison and Farm, was a medium security prison located in Henning, Tennessee, which closed in 1999.

13. **Furlough** - a leave of absence granted to a soldier or prisoner; also: a document authorizing such a leave of absence.

14. **Havoc** - wide and general destruction: devastation: great confusion and disorder.

15. **Hellhole** - a place of extreme misery or squalor.

16. **Holding Tank** – slang for a prison cell or enclosure, used for temporarily detaining prisoners while they are being processed.

17. **Incarcerated** - to put in prison: to subject to confinement.

18. **Mayhem** - willful and permanent deprivation of a bodily member resulting in the impairment of a person's fighting ability b: willful and permanent crippling, mutilation, or disfigurement of any part of the body: needless or willful damage or violence.

19. **Music Row** – a business district in Nashville, TN developed in the 1950s as a center of the recording industry. The location houses many recording studios, music producers and various elements of the musical recording industry.

20. **Opening Act-** The performance before the main event or act.

21. **Parole** - a conditional release of a prisoner serving an indeterminate or unexpired sentence.

22. **Post Conviction Relief** – a federal or state prisoner, attacking the constitutionality of his sentence, may move the court which imposed the sentence to vacate, set aside or correct the same.

23. **Prison Security Levels** – the security levels used by the Division of Prisons are maximum, close, medium, and minimum. Security levels are determined by the design and unique features of the prison, the level of staffing, and the operating procedures. Maximum security is the most restrictive level of confinement and minimum security is the least restrictive. The prison security level is an indicator of the extent to which an offender who is assigned to that facility is separated from the civilian community.

24. **Reception Center** - the area designed for acceptance, accountability, processing, and classification of new prisoners.

25. **Rendezvous** - a place appointed for assembling or meeting; a place of popular resort: haunt; a meeting at an appointed place and time.

26. **Safety Valve** - something that relieves the pressure of overcrowding.

27. **Spar** - a movement of offense or defense in boxing: a sparring match or session.

28. **Strenuous** - vigorously active: energetic; fervent, zealous: marked by or calling for energy or stamina: arduous.

29. **The Farm** – any one of the three prison/farms located throughout the state of TN. All of which are minimum or medium security level prisons, with emphasis in industrial and farm related activities.

30. **The Walls** – colloquial terminology for the Tennessee State Penitentiary which became operational in 1831 for both men and women. It is located in Nashville, TN and ceased operations in June of 1992.

31. **Turney Center** - Turney Center Industrial Prison and Farm is located in Only, Tennessee and is a time-building institution with emphasis on industry.

BIBLIOGRAPHY

Bartlett, John, <u>Bartlett's Familiar Quotations</u>, 17th ed., Little, Brown and Company, 2002

Morris, Tom Ph.D., <u>Philosophy for Dummies</u>, IDG Books Worldwide, Inc., 1999

<u>Langenscheidt's Pocket Dictionary Merriam Webster</u>, 1997 ed., Langenscheidt

<u>The New Webster's Concise Dictionary</u>, 2003 ed., Trident Press International

<u>The Oxford Dictionary of Quotations</u>, 3rd ed., Oxford University Press, 1979

<u>The Thompson Chain-Reference Bible (KJV)</u>, 4th ed., B.B. Kirkbride Bible Co. Inc. 1964

Made in the USA
Middletown, DE
28 April 2015